SALT

Flavouring the Moral and Spiritual Climate of Our World

SALT

Flavouring the Moral and Spiritual Climate of Our World

Copyright © David Mainse and Sarah Shaheen Stowell

Published by Crossroads Christian Communications Inc.
P.O. Box 5100, Burlington, ON   L7R 4M2

Design and Layout: Michael Moon
Cover Design: Todd Neilson
Printed by Canadian Printing Resources

ISBN   0 - 921702 - 97 - 3

Dedication

This book is dedicated to Dr. Don Reimer, founder and chairman of Reimer World Express Corporation.

Dr. Reimer is a man of vision who believed in the "salt project" from its beginning in 2007. He helped provide travel and accommodations, as well as meeting rooms and meals, for a large number of ministers and priests in many cities and towns across Canada.

In 2008, Dr. Reimer once again took up the challenge of helping with the publishing this book and its distribution to more than 10,000 church leaders from the Atlantic to the Pacific, and from the United States border to the Arctic. Thank you, Dr. Don Reimer, for being "salt" to our country.

Contents

Foreword

What do the Apostle John, Moses, Joshua, Caleb, as well as Sir Winston Churchill and the 2008 United States presidential candidate John McCain all have in common? They all flourished after they had reached the Biblical life expectancy of three score and ten (70). I'm in my eighth decade and filled with energy. I think I'm smarter than I used to be. Some would claim that's not saying much – and sometimes I agree!

In 2007, I had a dream. I remembered the words of the prophet Joel, used as the text for the sermon of St. Peter at the birthday of the Church: *"And it shall come to pass...your old men shall dream dreams..."* (Joel 2:28). No, I was not sleeping. This was a wide-awake dream, and one that required action.

In 2003, I retired as president of the not-for-profit Crossroads Christian Communications Incorporated and as chairman of the Crossroads Television System (CTS). An officially retired person needs lots of help, particularly when he has a dream to fill. Much help came from Valerie Battaglia who typed and retyped this manuscript, deciphering my handwriting as she has done for more than 30 years.

I want to thank Crossroads' new president, Rev. Ron Mainse, and his team, for their moral and financial support, assisting me to cross the continent – meeting in cities and towns with ministers, priests and Christian workers. Crossroads gave me the gift of Rev. David Rutledge, its Director of Ministry Relations. David set up the luncheons, inspired and coaxed Christian leaders to attend, and made it easy for me to show up.

I also want to thank Dr. Don Reimer, Sidney Harkema (a former Crossroads board member), Roy Ferguson, and Don and Fay Simmonds for donations to the cause. Thanks also to Rev. Mark Griffin who selected and "salted" 30 daily devotionals from my book, *Going the Extra Smile*. Editor Karen Stiller gave valuable insights on content. Finally, Karen Stowell and Phil Thatcher, editors of the *Crossroads Compass* magazine, made the final revisions. I owe them all – and others – great gratitude.

In addition, I want to thank my granddaughter Sarah Shaheen Stowell, B.Th., who gave birth to my great-granddaughter, Aliyah Joy Stowell, on March 13, 2007, in Burlington, Ontario. Because Sarah had completed her undergraduate studies and was a stay-at-home, full-time mother, I asked her and her husband Jordan if they would help "Grandpa" with this project.

Sarah carefully sorted through hundreds of statements from church leaders and selected the quotes included in this book. The viewpoint of this young couple in their 20s is essential input for a man in his 70s. Sarah has written some of the content in the book and, therefore, "Sarah" appears before most of her contributions.

David Mainse

What This Book Is About

In writing this book, we asked pastors, priests and church workers from across Canada to respond to four questions. You will find those questions, in the exact format used by the clergy for their responses, in Appendix A. We encourage readers to complete the exercise.

Here are the four questions:

1. How did Jesus model His SALT message?
   "You are the salt of the earth; but if the salt loses its flavour, how shall it be seasoned? It is then good for nothing but to be thrown out and trampled underfoot by men." ~ Matthew 5:13

2. What is the balance of the prophetic role of the Church in culture and the call to be loving and kind?

3. As it is believed best for the Church not to endorse specific political parties or candidates, please respond to this question: What are the rights and responsibilities of the Church in the political process?

4. In the balance of the prophetic role of the practical application of truth to daily life, what can the pastors, shepherds, spiritual fathers and mothers do to reverse the moral and social deconstruction of our historical Christian values?

Introduction

I'm writing this during the winter of 2008 in the cozy comfort of an isolated home in Ontario cottage country. The trees form a winter wonderland. It all looks so serene and so beautiful. All should be right with the world. But it's not. The little three-letter word "sin" has messed with God's original plans.

The Church is God's great creation. Our Lord said, *"I will build My Church and the gates of hell shall not prevail against it"* (Matthew 16:18b ESV). He also states, *"My sheep hear My voice; I know them and they follow Me"* (John 10:27 NIV). In calling His followers sheep, Jesus was not complimenting our high intelligence. The compliment is found instead in the words *"...they follow Me."* I believe I'm doing just that in this unworthy effort.

My wife Norma-Jean and I lived for many years on the farm where she was born. We had sheep that knew their master's voice. It wasn't my voice, it was Norma's. When she called, they came running. As she held them in her arms as lambs, they learned her voice. Norma was there for them when they got up in the morning and when they retired at night. Her presence was constant.

God is omnipresent, always there. I'm confident that our Great Shepherd leads us into green pastures and beside the still waters. He restores our souls. He prepares a table for us. May this book be a tiny reminder that His goodness and mercy are following us (Psalm 23:6).

In 1962, I began a weekly telecast called *Crossroads*. In 1973, the children's *Circle Square* television program was launched. Then in 1977, I was joined by Father Bob MacDougall, a Roman Catholic priest; Rev. Al Reimers, an Anglican priest; Rev. Jim Poynter, a Free Methodist minister; and Rev. Don Osborne and Rev. Clyde Williamson, both Pentecostals, in launching Canada's first daily Christian TV ministry. Later we were joined by Rev. Gordon Williams, a minister with the United Church of Canada.

The Toronto Star reported this unusual menagerie of clergy with these words: "While they come from different denominations, don't let them fool you, they're really all the same." Was that intended positively or negatively? We chose to believe that it was an acknowledgement of an answer to Jesus' prayer: *"I do not pray for these alone [the apostles] but also for those who will believe in Me through their word; that they all may be one as You, Father, are in Me, and I in You; that they also may be one in Us, that the world may believe that You sent Me"* (John 17:20-21).

(from left to right) Arthur Blessit, who travelled the world carrying a cross; David Mainse; Fr. Bob MacDougall (Roman Catholic priest); Rev. Gordon Williams (United Church Minister); Rev. Al Reimers (Anglican); Rev. Don Osborne (Pentecostal); Rev. Jim Poynter (Free Methodist).

While only the angels keep true records of those who believe, the Crossroads/*100 Huntley Street* ministry has recorded 8,265,148 calls to the prayer lines from January 1, 1980 to March 2008. Rev. Don Osborne estimates that there had been about 1,000,000 calls prior to 1980. Many of these callers said that, for the first time, they were making a firm decision to truly follow Christ. Many others registered a renewal or a reconfirmation of their personal faith. The ripple effect of this visible demonstration of an answer to Jesus' prayer is mind-boggling to me.

Through the years, the *Circle Square* children's TV program has morphed into year-round camps. Thousands of youth have committed their lives to Christ at these nine Circle Square Ranches across Canada. The records indicate that approximately 60 percent of the children and teens attending had no prior church connection. Another highly effective outreach for children was the *Kingdom Adventure* program which was produced and distributed in more than 50 countries.

The *Crossroads Creation Series* was the very first Christian television series in the Soviet Union. It was designed carefully and prayerfully to create doubt in the minds of atheists. Other television programs have been produced in 18 languages other than English.

There have been Christian pavilions in four World Expositions, beginning with Vancouver in 1986. At the '92 Expo in Seville, Spain, over 53,000 visitors registered new decisions to follow Christ. Msgr. Carlos Amigo, Archbishop of Seville (now a cardinal) and also cousin to King Carlos, expressed with tears, "My people need this message."

For several years, I had the opportunity to serve as a judge in the *International Templeton Prize for Progress in Religion*. Sir John Templeton watched *100 Huntley Street* regularly from his home in the Bahamas. Well-known broadcaster and businessman Ted Rogers also served as a judge. One year, the prize was given to Roman Catholic intellectual Michael Novak. His faith in Christ underlies his concepts for the best in human freedom and the ideal human government. Novak's writings became like a "Bible" to playwright, Václav Havel. The Czech leader met weekly with a prayer group to study Novak's work. Havel wielded a torch cutting through the Iron Curtain. The following is my paraphrase of Havel's comments: "We must serve the people. We must serve future generations. Our inspiration is founded in a moral conscience. We must express our responsibility through action to benefit everyone."

Back in the mid-70s, Dr. John Redekop, professor of Political Science at Sir Wilfrid Laurier University in Waterloo, wrote a book on Christians and politics. The dust jacket on his book had a pair of glasses with portions of the American flag as the lenses. This Mennonite professor, deeply committed to Christ, opened my eyes to the folly of seeing our responsibilities as Christians through nationalistic glasses. It was obvious that political decisions, for some, were motivated to a great extent by a commitment to a worldview shaped by self-centred or nation-centred thoughts, rather than by a Biblical Christ-centred understanding of political reality.

I offer these memories and experiences as examples to you of how we can learn from each other in our Christian walk, and how we need each other in order to be more effective as salt in the world. That's what this book is designed to do. Together we will explore what it means to be salt, offer encouragement and instruction, and draw on the insights of Christian leaders from various denominations across Canada. We hope it will help you become even more salty!

In the process of creating this book, Rev. David Rutledge and I conducted meetings all across the country with Canadian clergy. We met with them. We asked them questions. And we listened to their answers. What I saw – overwhelmingly – were men and women of God who see that it is time for a change. Are you ready for change?

The final gathering of the "SALT" tour in Hay River, N.W.T. April, 2008. (Left to right, back row): Georgina Bassett, Shelene Giraldi, Lucas Giraldi, Pastor Dean Steel, Bishop Jack Sperry, Rev. David Mainse, Jane Groenewegen. (Left to right, front row): Chief Alec Sunrise, Rev. Vivian Smith & Father Bernie Black.

Chapter 1

Just How Salty Are You?

My wife Norma-Jean and I spend the winters in Florida where we have a mobile home in a senior's park. There is a chapel service every Tuesday in the clubhouse. In our area, there are almost 50 parks with chapels like this one, under the leadership and inspiration of Dr. Melvin Maxwell, a retired university president from Indiana. John Maxwell, the famous motivational speaker, is his son.

In March of this year, one chapel service featured retired Pastor Robert Curle of Ohio. He summed up his pastoral ministry from the "Good Samaritan" story (Luke 10:30-37). Robert always wanted to be the Good Samaritan. Frustrated in this effort, he went to fervent prayer. The still small voice he heard surprised and, at first, even disappointed him: "You can't be the Good Samaritan. That's My job. Your calling is to be the innkeeper. I'll deliver the naked, the wounded and the half-dead to you. I'll do the initial bandaging, pour on the oil and the wine, and bring them to you. I'll give you the finances to cover the expenses, but you must take care of them. And whatever more you spend, when I come again, I will repay you."

Now, that *is* salt. I'm absolutely sure that when Jesus comes, He *will* repay. Salt works in a way that is unseen and unheard. In fact, it disappeared in the soup I just had for lunch. But it certainly helped to make the soup very tasty!

As I look back over 50 years of ministry, I recognize that God has brought the wounded to me over and over again. I know that when He says, "You take care of this precious person," I must heed His voice. Yet I confess that, to my shame, I've often complained. Meanwhile, the innkeeper's wife is bathing the elderly shut-in or cooking for those who can't do so themselves.

Recently, Norma-Jean bathed an 85-year-old woman. The elderly woman thanked my wife profusely – and told me that I talk too much. Ouch! However, she needed money, and one good work I *could* do was visit the bank and come up with some cash to help her.

So I did just that. Norma-Jean and I were both salt in that situation, and God used our particular strengths and abilities to reach out to someone who needed help.

Being salt is an essential part of being a Christian. Jesus provided the first – and best – model of what being salty is all about. Compassion was the rule of thumb for the Son of God. He responded with tender loving care. Time and time again, He had opportunity to weigh in on the evils of Rome, but instead delivered stinging rebukes to the religious/political crowd in His own faith of Judaism. Christ was never tolerant of sin. Again and again, He called for repentance. He stressed this twice in Luke 13:1-5 while addressing the people's concern.

The Call To Repentance

An important part of our identity as salt in the modern world is calling for repentance, but it always requires compassion. For example, I am against abortion, not because of a conservative agenda, but because Jesus was conceived in the virgin's womb by the Holy Spirit. He was there from conception. The Scriptures teach that every person is precious to God, even in the womb (Psalm 139). God obviously views the yet-to-be-born as fully human. That little person has a totally unique DNA.

Former President Bill Clinton vetoed the partial birth abortion ban passed by the United States congress. I failed to understand his position until near the end of his book, *My Life*, where he states that about 100,000 years ago, the first human rose from all fours to stand upright. Did God really create us as a special creation in His own image? Or did we evolve solely from other life forms without His specific act of a new creation? Nowhere did Clinton mention God's involvement in creation.

I also oppose "same-sex marriage," not because of a conservative right-wing political position, and not because I don't love people unconditionally, but because ancient Church tradition always teaches one man and one woman only in marriage. The Scriptures declare that God made one man and one woman. Jesus quoted Moses on the issue, and that decides the issue for me (Genesis 2:24).

While I oppose certain actions, I am also *for* a multitude of positive initiatives. Some of those initiatives might even come from someone, or a group of people, with whom I might have difficulties in some areas. Nevertheless, I need to come on board and be a part of the engine, not just a trailer going along for the ride.

Murray Cantelon, a union leader from British Columbia (also the brother of former *100 Huntley Street* host Jim Cantelon) said, "The world is run by people who show up at the meetings." Sometimes the Church is rightfully accused by the world around us because we *don't* show up. We don't make our case in a well-reasoned civil manner. For example, there is a general perception that some Christians are not really interested in environmental issues. We have allowed open-line radio hosts, or (gulp) TV evangelists, to define who we are, instead of each of us individually – and all of us collectively.

The Scriptures teach that we don't own the planet. We are merely stewards. We are to take tender loving care of what God declared was *"good"* and *"very good"* (Genesis 1:10; 12; 18; 21; 25; 31). We know that *"the earth is the Lord's, and all its fullness..."* (Psalm 24:1). Our first job was as gardener. But that was paradise. Is it not all the more reason to take care of God's creation now?

As individuals, and as the Church, we need to take strong leadership in moral and social responsibilities. It is sin to fail to lead in issues such as reducing poverty, meeting the needs of widows, orphans and single mothers, fighting injustice, curing disease, and reducing pollution. The Scriptures say, *"Therefore, to him who knows to do good and does not do it, to him it is sin"* (James 4:17). After all, that is what being salt is all about.

Take a moment to reflect:

1. List areas where you can be salty.

2. Think about areas where people you know are leading "salt projects." Write them down. Are there ways you can become involved and be an enthusiastic and salty follower of Jesus?

Chapter 2

Jesus as Salt

To discover more about our ultimate inspiration for being salt in the world, we explored our first question with Christian leaders from across Canada and from across denominations. Their answers help us better understand how to follow the model of Jesus Christ in being salt so we can flavour a hurting world. As a reminder, here is the first question we asked: **How did Jesus model his SALT message?** (Matthew 5:13). Before we turn to their answers, let's remind ourselves of the very nature of Jesus.

Jesus: Our Salt Model

Sarah's Comments:

Jesus was a Man of the people. He lived, breathed and ate with the ordinary people of His day. His closest companions did not come from elite society, but from the ranks of regular working people. He was earthy and real; there was nothing counterfeit about Him. Jesus' essence was love and humility. He flavoured culture with grace and truth, and was willing to pay the ultimate sacrifice for His message.

As we reflect on the message and method of this first-century God-Man, we must ask ourselves if we are the salt of the earth in the way Jesus was to His culture – the way that He desires His followers to be. And what exactly does it mean to be salt? How can we emulate Jesus? Or perhaps a better way of putting it is, how can Jesus live His life in us? How can we, in a time that is so very different from Jesus' era, fulfill this mandate?

Think about salt for a moment. It is not the dominant ingredient in food, yet it enhances the flavour. Likewise, the Church is at its best when it permeates society but does not dominate. Matthew 5:13 reads: *"You are the salt of the earth. But if the salt loses its saltiness, how can it be made salty again? It is no longer good for anything, except to be thrown out and trampled by men"* (NIV). If we who claim to follow Christ no longer have influence on our society then, essentially, we are considered good for nothing. Our message – and we ourselves – will first be marginalized and eventually discarded altogether.

Culture has changed dramatically since Jesus' time but the hearts and motives of people have stayed the same. The message of Jesus is for all times, and wholly transferable to us today. We must permeate the earth as salt. We must flavour society, preserving what is good, kind, loving, and true for everyone's benefit.

David's Comments:

If you are a grandparent, you will understand my joy at working with Sarah, my granddaughter. Sarah has summarized the fascinating insights of 18 of the Church leaders we interviewed, followed by direct quotes from 27 more on this very important first question.

Canadian Clergy Offer a Salt Summary

Jesus' focus was on the priorities of the Kingdom of God for those who would receive it, and on the transformation of people's hearts, minds, motives, life and priorities. He spent the majority of His time investing in the lives of 12 of His closest friends – mobilizing His disciples to carry on His message after He left. [1]

Jesus moved amongst the people at a grassroots level. He challenged the entrenched powers with passion, courage and cultural awareness.[2] Jesus did not gloss over the issues that people dealt with, as so many of us do. He spoke to the real needs and pressure points that existed in people's lives.[3] We cannot pretend that people don't have real sticky and painful issues. Messy situations exist. Jesus wasn't afraid to deal with them and our leaders must be willing to

---

1   Rick Lamothe and Donna Boisvert, Sequoia Community Church, Barrhaven, ON

2   Wes Mcleod, Director of Faith Political Interface Program, Ottawa, ON

3   Leo Van Arragon, Principal of Redeemer Christian High School, Nepean, ON

speak to those needs. As St. Paul said, *"Follow my example, as I follow the example of Christ"* (1 Corinthians 11:1 NIV).

Perhaps the most important way Jesus modelled His salt message was by taking time for His own relationship with God.[4] It was not people or pressure that motivated Him; it was His "solitary place" relationship with the Father (Mark 1:35) that fuelled Him.[5]

Jesus was anchored in His message and actions because He was anchored in the Father. He was not swayed by emotions or the changing tide; He was solid in his portrayal of the Kingdom of God. Without Him taking time to commune with the Father, it would have been impossible for Him to fulfill His mission on earth. Although there was never a time He was less than 100 percent God, He lived as 100 percent Man, filled with the Holy Spirit.

An important part of Jesus' salt identity was His advocacy for change – He never left things the way He found them.[6] Jesus challenged both the misunderstandings and the false teaching that existed within Judaism.[7] He challenged the injustices of society, both within the temple and outside its walls.[8] He was never afraid to touch a leper or speak to a harlot. He was open with all classes of people – men, women and children.

By His very presence, Jesus stirred the pot and flavoured society with deliverance, healings, and resurrection. He modelled truth as life-reality.[9] Opinion polls or opposition did not affect him. He continued to proclaim the Good News in the face of religiosity and conformity. The change that Jesus advocated was one that began in the heart and not in the external world.[10] The world-changer Marshall McLuhan wrote that Jesus was the only fully-integrated person in human history.

Jesus used the method of parables and story-telling to illustrate a

---

4   Rev. Lorna Casselman, Senior Pastor of Long Sault Pentecostal Church, Long Sault, ON

5   Rev. Kerry Kronberg, Sunnyside Wesleyan Church, Ottawa, ON

6   Rev. Mark J. Redner, Leader of Standing in the Gap and Pastor of West Carleton Christian Assembly, Ottawa, ON

7   Jan Kupecz, Canadian National Christian Foundation, Ottawa, ON

8   Colin Cleugh, Calvary Pentecostal Church, Gananoque, ON

9   Ruben Dietrich, Kingston, ON

10   Roger Armbruster, Director of Canada Awakening Ministries, Niverville, MB

salt message to the people. Instead of using high-sounding theological terms to relay Kingdom truths, He used stories. The parables would play over and over again in the people's minds in a way that merely stating facts could never have achieved. Jesus' parables were complex enough to convey eternal truths, yet simple enough for children to grasp.

The love that Jesus embodied was obvious to all around Him. It was proven by His willingness to associate with outcasts and people who had been deemed unclean by society. It was specifically those whom the religious leaders looked down upon that Jesus took the greatest care to love. He was always available for people.[11] He spent time with them and made serving them His life's work. Clearly, His life was His ministry, and His ministry was His life.[12] He created a new community that was in the business of restoration, rather than retribution.[13] This Kingdom community valued relationships and principles over the letter of the Law, and Jesus' followers were *interdependent,* instead of *independent.[14]*

Jesus lived according to what His Father wanted Him to do. He was in tune with His Father and, as a result, did not depart from His Father's will.[15] He loved deeply – laying down His life for others. He helped broadly – healing the sick, feeding the poor and welcoming the broken. He spoke clearly with a message that was not diluted by cultural norms and expectations.[16]

Love was something that Jesus lived, and still lives today. He is love, and His love is contagious. The *"King of kings"* got down on His knees to wash the feet of His friends. It is almost unfathomable. This humble act was deeply moving to His disciples as they watched it unfold. These followers had been shown love in action. And really, there is no such thing as love *without* action. After all, the world will know Christ's disciples by their love.[17] Jesus' ultimate act of love is, of course, the sacrifice of His life for the entire world. Jesus died for

---

11   Rod Daly, Saint John, NB
12   Pastor Dannie Brown, Worship Pastor of Marysville Baptist Church, Fredericton, NB
13   Alan Simpson, Surrey Pastors Network, Surrey, BC
14   Ian Lopez, Surrey, BC
15   Pastor Maria Collett, Edmonton Centre Victory Church, Edmonton, AB
16   Pastor David McElhinney, River Valley Wesleyan Church, Saint John, NB
17   Cornelius Buller, Executive Director of Urban Youth Adventures, Winnipeg, MB

us so we could live for Him.

Here are some more answers and insights from Christian leaders. As you read, consider how you can be salt in your part of the world.

1. How did Jesus model His SALT message?
(As mentioned in Matthew 5:13.)

"His focus was on the priorities of the Kingdom of God to those who would receive it. His focus was on the transformation of people's hearts, minds, motives, lives and priorities."

~ Rick Lamothe, Lead Pastor of Sequoia Community Church, Barrhaven, ON

"Jesus impacted everyone whom He touched…. He met spiritual and physical needs."

~ Rev. Winnie Forte, Deacon at St. Paul's Anglican Church, Kingston, ON

"…[Jesus] took time for His relationship with God…. His message was not changed by whoever He met or whatever He did."

~ Rev. Lorna Casselman, Senior Pastor of Long Sault Pentecostal Church, Long Sault, ON

"People did not drive Jesus. His 'solitary place' relationship with the Father fuelled Him (Mark 1:35)…. Jesus gathered a Kingdom people. It was their perfect love movement that was deeply healing to those in the society of the day."

~ Rev. Kerry Kronberg, Sunnyside Wesleyan Church, Ottawa, ON

"Boldness without compromise."

~ John Forstner, Queen of Peace Roman Catholic prayer group, Saint John, NB

"He modelled His salt message by challenging His disciples to look beyond the blessings of God to their responsibility on society."

~ Anonymous

"He went into all the world with the Gospel, associating with those from all walks of life – not just the religious but the secular – sharing with all the Lord's truth."

~ Rev. Bill Bresnahan, Grace United Church, Gananoque, ON

"Jesus modelled by example – basin and towel. He challenged the injustices of society outside and inside the Church."

~ Colin Cleugh, Calvary Pentecostal Church, Gananoque, ON

"Jesus was never afraid to touch a leper or speak to a harlot. He was open with all classes, both men and women, as well as children. There was no hypocrisy in Jesus."

~ Rev. John and Marilyn Craig, Amherstview Community Church, Amherstview, ON

"...Faithfulness and obedience in the face of much opposition."

~ Rick Chase, Gateway Baptist Church, Surrey, BC

"Jesus, by His very presence, stirred up the pot and flavoured society – deliverance, healings, resurrection; truth as life reality, and not just academic."

~ Ruben Dietrich, Kingston, ON

"He modelled a non-dictatorial and non-materialistic lifestyle."

~ Pastor Ted Boodle, Westwinds Community Church, Surrey, BC

"[Jesus] included a 'zealot' in His disciples – willing to engage those with strong political views."

~ Rev. John Allsop, St. James United Church, Waterdown, ON

"He came without fear; for example, His words to the rich young ruler. Another example: the whip in the temple.... Shows advocacy and His desire to speak out for those who couldn't speak for themselves."

~ Chris and Jenn Banas, Spruce Grove Community Church, Edmonton, AB

"*Preservation* and *flavour* - At the wedding in Cana, He *preserved* the dignity of the family on the one hand, and extended and brought value to the celebration.... It's interesting to note that the young couple were not aware of His kindness until later, as so often happens when He is at work."
~ *David Lee Pong, People's Church, Edmonton, AB*

"He did not depart from His Father's will."
~ *Pastor Maria Collett, Edmonton Centre Victory Church, Edmonton, AB*

"...Credibility tied to integrity. What He thought, what He said and what He did were always one – no discrepancies."
~ *Norah Kennedy, Director of Pregnancy Care Centre, Edmonton, AB*

"Jesus spoke of both salt and light – light to dispel darkness; salt to give flavour, meaning and taste. Salt dissolves and permeates what it touches. Jesus does this in ministry, sending apostles and disciples to evangelize...."
~ *Fr. Peter B. Coughlin, Pastor of St. Andrew's Roman Catholic Church, Oakville, ON*

"He loved *deeply* – laying down His life for others. He helped *broadly* – healing the sick, feeding the poor, and welcoming the broken. He spoke *clearly* – focussing on others."
~ *David McElhinney, River Valley Wesleyan Church, Saint John, NB*

"Jesus knew why He was here! And He courageously and persistently went about doing it. He was not affected by opinion polls or opposition. He defended the poor and the disadvantaged. He proclaimed the Good News of the Kingdom in the face of religiosity and conformity."
~ *Anonymous*

"He gave people room to respond."
~ *Keith Joyce, Christ Church Cathedral (Anglican), Fredericton, NB*

"Incarnation – the Word became flesh and lived among us. Jesus related the universal truth of God to every individual and situation He came into contact with and He searched out opportunities to speak and live the Good News."

~ *John Paul Westin, St. Thomas Anglican Church, St. John's, NL*

"He salted as needed...recognized the existence of sin and went to the oppressed. He came as one modelling servanthood.... He opposed Rome through His martyrdom (1 Peter 2:20)."

~ *Dr. Blayne Banting, Briercrest College and Seminary, Caronport, SK*

"Jesus was hard on those who knew better, but soft on those who did not.... He didn't bring condemnation but challenged people to stop sinning. He was willing to pay the price for His convictions even unto death."

~ *Rick Wells, Lead Pastor of The Creek Community Church, Stoney Creek, ON*

"He lived a life that brought redemption to a lost and broken culture mired in religious ritual."

~ *Pastor Stephen Whyte, Paramount Drive Alliance Church, Stoney Creek, ON*

"Jesus was an advocate of change. He never left things the way He found them. He met with crowds but was never afraid to speak or meet with just one person. He associated with people the religious would not."

~ *Rev. Mark J. Redner, Leader of Standing in the Gap and Pastor of West Carleton Christian Assembly, Ottawa, ON*

Chapter 3

The Longest Salt Message

Sarah's Comments:

Jesus' definitive teaching on how to be salt is found in His famous Sermon on the Mount as recorded in Matthew 5-7. These passages of Scripture contain everything we need to know to be the sort of salty Christians God wants us to be.

The beautiful thing about the Sermon on the Mount is that it is not a cumbersome list of rules and regulations. It is a breath of fresh air. This manual for Christian living is based on principles, rather than rules. It is intended to bring freedom and joy to the lives of those who seek to live by the standards set out by Christ. Our Lord would not have set out impossible goals. By identifying with the Cross daily and appropriating God's grace, we can look back with surprise – one day at a time – to see that it worked so very well indeed.

Church culture has perfected their method of talking about doing the right thing. Statistics show, in general, that the vast majority of the income of the Church is spent within its four walls and not on things like community outreach and missions. The sermon that Jesus preached flies in the face of such an inward-focussed culture and requires that one give sacrificially to be His true disciple. The Church, as the Body of Christ, must give sacrificially to authentically live out the calling Christ gave to the Church.

The Sermon on the Mount was counter-cultural when Jesus first shared it on that Galilean mountainside. Today, the message is just as counter-cultural in our fast-paced global village. Meekness and mercy – and values like them – do not top the list of attributes that the average person wishes to possess.

As followers of Christ, we must ask ourselves if we truly believe what He preached in His famous sermon. If the answer is yes, then an attitude adjustment is required for the Church as a whole.

It is exciting to imagine how society could drastically change if we truly abandoned our North American materialism and reached higher for the things of God.

David's Comments:

In 1995, I wrote a book called *Going the Extra Smile* with the help of my son Reynold. It was a daily devotional, based on the Sermon on the Mount. That sermon is Christ's longest recorded message. The entire message teaches what Jesus means when He says to be salt. In fact, at the back of this book, you will find one month's worth of daily meditations adapted from *Going the Extra Smile*. I invite you to commit to reading one each day for 30 days. They are designed to help each of us on our quest to live the salt life more fully.

Salt itself is the stuff of history. It is so vital to human survival that wars have been fought over it; empires have been founded on it and simply collapsed without it. Civilizations have grown up around it. Humankind realized from the earliest days that, without salt, we perish. Without it in our bodies, the delicate balance between salt and water is upset, and death occurs through dehydration.

The function of God's people, living in a world that disowns Him, is to prevent society from going completely bad. We are given the responsibility of preserving all that is good, kind, loving, pure and true. While the emphasis here is salt, there is an interesting connection with "light." Light must shine in order to show salt's impact. Immediately after His salt statement, Jesus said, *"Let your light so shine before men, that they may see your good works, and glorify your Father in heaven"* (Matthew 5:16).

What Salt Can Do

The world will either be a brighter or darker place because of our influence – or lack of impact – on it. We need to hit the switch and let our lights shine brightly. But how can we possibly be light in such a dark world? Most of us feel that our influence is little and our light does not make a dramatic difference. How wrong we are.

Light is always more powerful than darkness. An epitaph I once read proclaimed: "There isn't enough darkness in all the world to put out the light of a single candle."

Take a moment at your next opportunity to truly notice a sunrise. Before the sun actually appears, its influence is felt. Slowly, almost mystically, a subtle change begins to take place in the world. Darkness loosens its grip and dissolves into day. As the sun rises higher in the sky, all the darkness is gone. The world of fear and unknown is soon filled with beautiful trees, running brooks, and towering mountains. What a difference the light makes. The despair of night is overwhelmed by the dawning of light.

If you love good, you represent good. Just as a lighthouse shines in the darkness – giving light, guidance, and warning – this world is in great need of people who will demonstrate what is good and acceptable. We may not realize that, with each drop of kindness or cruelty, there are waves of ever-widening circles that impact many lives. We are either bringing light to the world or allowing the darkness to continue.

As believers, we are called the light of the world. There is no better place to shine or "to salt" than in our homes. As parents, we need to seriously consider our relationships with our children, especially during the formative years. Our relationships with them will greatly affect their adult relationships with God. Even as you strive to represent God to the world, don't forget to represent Him well to your children and model the ways you want them to be.

Salting Society

Sarah's Comments:

I don't think that Jesus is happy with the current North American Church culture. But there is still so much hope for the Church. We have the potential to radically change our culture for Christ. Imagine a church that spends Sunday inside the church building, and every other day in the community. Imagine a church that reduces expenditures on its building in order to invest most of this money in helping the community. Think about a church that opens its doors to host community events and takes a special interest in the down-and-out of their community. Can you picture a church that encourages each member to get involved in ministry outside the walls? What would a church be like that raises money for a local charity? Or a church that gets involved in helping renovate a single mom's home or offers her reasonably priced or free daycare services?

The list could go on and on. Of course, there are churches in Canada already doing these things. When the Church changes from the inside out, and begins to give of itself sacrificially, society will see the Church – and our Christian faith – in a whole new light. If every church in Canada could take on this Christ-like attitude, we could truly change the landscape of Canadian culture. Idealistic? Perhaps. But we, as followers of Christ, believe that nothing is too big for God.

The old method of expecting people to grace the doors of our churches before we go to them is not working. When we preach the raw and undiluted message of Christ, and truly become an example of Christ's love in the community, then lives will be changed and society will be impacted. The message is not new; it is an old one. But we must offer this age-old truth in a fresh new way.

What we offer, how we present it, and the words we use, are all part of our prophetic voice in contemporary Canada. Next, let's consider what it means to have a prophetic voice.

*"When the Church changes from
the inside out, and begins to give of itself
sacrificially, society will see the Church –
and our Christian faith –
in a whole new light."*

Chapter 4

Balance in the Body:
Unity, Kindness and the Prophetic Voice

Ever since the birth of the Church, believers were to be the voice of truth to the world. Our mandate is God-given. Sometimes our prophetic voice and the call to be loving and kind are out of balance. One is lost in pursuit of the other. The Church needs to ask itself, "Where is compassion and kindness without truth?" and "Where is truth without compassion and kindness?"

In the third year of my ordained ministry, I learned a valuable lesson. I was a pastor in a community with a population of 5,000. I advertised in the local newspaper that I would be preaching on "the washing of the blood of Christ."

I heard that a fellow minister in town had mocked me, saying, "Can you imagine taking a bath in blood?" I was hurt, and I nursed those hurts for several weeks. Hurt turned into resentment, and I deliberately avoided this pastor. By God's grace, I barely avoided retaliation in my pulpit. But the Holy Spirit was faithful and brought me to repentance. Jesus poured the oil of the Holy Spirit into my hurts and once again washed away my sin in His blood.

About six months passed and I heard that this pastor's dear wife was diagnosed with a fast-moving form of cancer. I knew what I had to do. I called him and asked if I could come to his home to visit and pray. There, kneeling together beside his wife's bed, we wept and prayed with our arms around each other. Our doctrinal differences were not resolved, but they were subordinated to God's infinite love in the face of tragedy. The woman passed away shortly after. I lost track of this pastor when we both moved away.

Years later, I picked up a copy of a community newspaper and discovered someone had written something completely false about my wife Norma-Jean. Guess who came to our defence in an article testifying about the utter falseness of the accusation? It was that pastor from long ago who defended our integrity. While our differences remained, we – by God's grace – respected each other. When we are loving and kind to each other within the Body of Christ, our prophetic voice to the world is even stronger.

Sarah's Comments:

There are many questions to be explored in considering the prophetic role of the Church. The culture we live in is very quick to label institutions intolerant if we go against the grain of popular culture and thought. But can the Church be tolerant of a morally decaying society, while still maintaining a high view of truth?

Disunity is a major factor in silencing the prophetic voice of the Church. My grandfather's story about the pastor who hurt him, and later defended him, helps show how the Church as a whole can overcome doctrinal differences to present a united front.

There are too many little voices out there, but not one big resounding voice from the Church in our country. Denominations have goals that pertain to their individual needs. Parachurch ministries do the same. These goals may have the appearance of disunity, especially in the eyes of non-believing individuals.

I believe we must be honest and truly evaluate how much of a presence Christianity has in this nation. We all know that many of our laws, and even democracy itself, come from Judeo-Christian principles, but I challenge Christians to pay attention to our country today – to the voice of the media, entertainment, and even the talk around the watercooler at work. Does Christianity have a voice and a presence in our postmodern society? Is that voice respected? Does the voice come from a Church that is aware and honest about its own failures and need for forgiveness?

Prophetic words to our generation would be so much more effective if they came from a repentant Church. It is time to challenge ourselves, our people and our churches to truly examine our hearts and the motives of our "prophetic words." This is where love and kindness must rule supreme.

David's Comments:

I learned in a unique way that followers of Jesus can still be one Body. David Demian, an Egyptian surgeon now living in Vancouver, leads a group I participate in called *Watchmen for the Nations*. God gave the group a call and a revolutionary vision. Remember "The Ship of the Damned"? This ship was carrying 900 Jewish men, women and children who were fleeing the Nazi scourge. The United States, Cuba and, to our shame, Canada, turned it and its passengers back to Europe and the death camps.

More than 600 people perished. But some of the children survived. In November of 2000, these survivors were brought to Canada by the "watchmen." David asked me if I would speak words of repentance for the sin of rejecting the refugees, on behalf of the Church in Canada. My first reaction was, "No, I have no right to represent the Church of Canada."

Then came my change of heart, prompted by a gathering in September of that same year. The historical churches of Toronto staged a celebration of 2,000 years since the birth of Jesus. I was asked to host and chair the gathering in Nathan Phillips Square. It was my honour to introduce the participants one-by-one. They included the Roman Catholic archbishop of Toronto and the Greek Orthodox archbishops, along with the bishops of other ancient churches and with the moderators of the reformation Protestant denominations. The newer non-liturgical churches were conspicuous by their absence.

Remember, I am an ordained minister with the Pentecostal Assemblies of Canada (PAOC). Now, there I was, hosting the great celebration of the incarnation with the Pentecostals, definitely in the minority among that gathering of thousands. What on earth was I doing there? I'm a television evangelist. We all know our reputation is not the greatest.

I thought of the counsel of my hero in the ministry, Rev. Tom Johnstone, a former general superintendent of the PAOC. He gave me this wise advice: "David, pure evangelism can never be tainted by a party spirit. It must transcend the denomination." As I stood in Nathan Phillips Square that day, I remembered David Demian's invitation to represent the Church before the Jewish survivors of the *St. Louis* ship.

On that September day, I finally asked the chairman of the organizational committee, the question that had been burning in my mind: "Why on earth would you invite me, of all people, to lead this celebration?" This Roman Catholic priest answered: "That's easy. You're the Canadian who best represents us all."

I was so dumbfounded, I spilled some of my coffee. I realized that the daily content of *100 Huntley Street* was making an impact. I knew immediately that I must say "yes" to leading the prayer of repentance at the *Watchmen for the Nations* event.

Reclaiming Hosea and Amos

Sarah's Comments:

A professor of mine, Dr. Gary Milley, taught me much about the prophets. The Old Testament has always seemed foreign to me. I have read historical fiction novels that are set in Old Testament times, and they paint a picture of simplicity and romance. But when I read actual sections from the Old Testament, it is more like a punch in the gut. It is raw and seems completely opposite to our culture today.

I believe the Old Testament has been very much misunderstood. Many people appreciate the poetic beauty and literary genius of Old Testament writings, but then question if there is anything modern humankind can glean from these daunting Scriptures. But one area of the Old Testament with which I can completely identify is the writings of the prophets. The prophets of the Old Testament have powerful and convicting messages to offer us.

Do you ever read something and find yourself nodding in agreement, and even saying "yes" out loud, to affirm your agreement with the author? This is what happens to me when I read the writings of Hosea and Amos. When I read of Hosea's almost pathetic and repetitive forgiveness of his adulterous wife, God's all-pursuing love becomes so clear. The story of Hosea is a poignant parallel of God's relationship with His people. We betray Him perpetually, and

He pursues us relentlessly.

One of the things that I learn from Hosea is God's steadfast love. It's not the "love" that we talk of in our culture. This love is sacrificial, unconditional, just and tough. *"For I desire steadfast love and not sacrifice, the knowledge of God rather than burnt offerings"* (Hosea 6:6 RSV). How do you *really* love God? I have struggled with this. Hosea's story brings attention both to God's unfailing love and our own unfaithfulness.

The love I feel for my daughter is so visceral. I would do anything for her protection and betterment. When she smiles at me, I am filled with joy. God is a little more mysterious. He isn't exactly sitting next to me on the floor while we colour and make silly faces! Exactly how does one love God? I think loving others with the same unconditional love that God models in Hosea is a good start. I have a long journey ahead of me in learning to love others and truly love God. So does the Church.

The prophets raised their voices to the people of God. And the Old Testament prophets have a message that we, as the people of God today, need to hear. We must be inwardly moved by the prophetic voice *before* turning our own prophetic voice on the world.

The book of Amos speaks of social justice and equality. It condemns God's people for overlooking the plight of those in need. It is truly a book for our times. We live in an affluent country. Canadians, even the poorest, have access to many services that those in other countries could only dream about. We live a cozy life and attend cozy churches.

Amos is blunt about the consequences of turning a blind eye to a brother or sister in need: *"Thus says the Lord: 'For three transgressions of Israel, and for four, I will not revoke the punishment; because they sell the righteous for silver, and the needy for a pair of shoes – they that trample the head of the poor into the dust of the earth, and turn aside the way of the afflicted...'"* (Amos 2:6,7 RSV). Isn't that what we do today? We buy products like coffee, shoes and clothing that we know might be unethically produced. Or we put our materialistic pursuits above the urgent and desperate needs of the poor. We are literally selling the needy for a pair of shoes. Amos made it clear that, unless God's people returned to a just society, punishment was around the corner. Maybe we are already living with some of that divine discipline? Christians must lead the charge for social justice. This is so much a part of Jesus' heart. If Jesus were here today, He would be standing up for the rights of those who are being left behind, just as He did in New Testament times. As a young evangelical Christian, I wish we were known more for our kindness and love than any other stereotype. Amos got it right.

A Voice That is Loving and Kind

The prophetic voice of the Church just cannot exist without the call to be loving and kind. Balance is needed. We have righteous anger, and we feel we should express it. We are in good company when we read the Old Testament, which is full of righteous anger. What we forget is that the righteous anger of the Old Testament was usually because of injustices in society. It's so easy to forget about the commandment that comes second only to loving God: *"Love your neighbour as yourself"* (Matthew 22:39). This is something we truly need to rediscover as a Church, and as the people of God.

When I lived in Toronto during my college years, I would pass homeless people on the streets and subway stations. I think the only thing I ever felt for them was pity, and perhaps a bit of superiority, as I wondered why they had made such a mess of their lives. Then for a class project, my husband Jordan and I interviewed Rudy, a homeless man. That interview forever changed the way I see the downtrodden of society. Rudy was intelligent. He had profound things to say. He had dignity, despite his addiction problems.

I discovered that Rudy was just like everyone else; he had feelings and thoughts and beliefs. He also expressed a faith in Jesus Christ that surprised me. Can we as Christians accept this man as a brother in Christ, despite his need for healing from addiction? This is where love and kindness come into play with the prophetic voice. It would be easy to preach at Rudy and think we've done him a great service: "Get your life together. Come to church. Shave your beard and stay sober…." Those words would be futile unless Rudy first received genuine love and compassion from us.

On the other end of the pendulum is the fear of speaking out. A lot of people would rather blend in with the crowd than speak words of truth. Do we care too much what the world thinks of us? As someone who is part of the 20-something generation, I can say that one of the biggest problems facing young adults who claim to be Christians is not big sin or lifestyle issues. It is an unwillingness to publicly live out our faith when it contradicts popular culture. Materialism is also high on the list. Having personal faith is great, but the prophetic voice gets lost somewhere between Wednesday's Bible study and Sunday's church service. We need to be a generation ready – if need be – to become unpopular for Christ.

David's Comments:

As Rev. David Rutledge and I crossed the country, meeting with Canadian clergy, we pondered their answers to our second question: "What is the balance of the prophetic role of the Church in culture and the call to be loving and kind?" Some of their answers will resonate with you. Some of them might not. Maybe you will disagree with some of the theology, but we think you will be challenged – and inspired. What we discovered is a Canadian clergy that is hungry for change. And change *is* coming.

2. What is the balance of the prophetic role of the Church in culture and the call to be loving and kind?

"We should be careful to make a clear balance between loving the people but challenging the system. Jesus vehemently challenged the pharisaic mechanism but loved individual Pharisees."

~ *Anonymous*

"We are needed as God's people to give of ourselves for the sake of others, and not fear the animosity and hostility and isolation this brings to us. We need to be honest about our mistakes, ask for forgiveness and be transparent."

~ *Rev. John and Marilyn Craig, Amherstview Community Church, Amherstview, ON*

"The Church must rise above the culture if the culture moves in a direction that contravenes the teachings of Christ, but we must do so in a manner that is persuasive, direct, yet tempered with love."

~ *Rev. Bill Bresnahan, Grace United Church, Gananoque, ON*

"The prophetic role of the Church is to speak and live God's Word to the world. Is that different from being loving and kind? Perhaps God's message is to be love and kindness. In the Old Testament, justice and righteousness were as much about speaking and acting for the oppressed and unloved as it was exposing the sins of the 'heathen.'"

~ *Ron Zehr, Surrey, BC*

"Repent of our uncritical participation in the fundamental goal of our culture: maximizing for ourselves the cozy pleasures."

~ *Cornelius Buller, Executive Director of Urban Youth Adventures, Winnipeg, MB*

"Biblical truth is often counter-cultural and anything counter-cultural is viewed as antagonistic. In John 4, Jesus explained how to deal with a sensitive situation. It appeared that it was normal for everyone to avoid this woman [at the well] because of lifestyle issues. Jesus, first of all, did not avoid her. So I would suppose that the Church ought not to avoid sensitive issues or situations or people. Secondly, Jesus addressed the lady with tenderness and care by establishing rapport with her where she was at. Thirdly, He spoke to her without compromise but with strength and tenderness."

~ *David Lee Pong, People's Church, Edmonton, AB*

"Confront culture with challenge for those things that destroy life and love – challenge the darkness and decay with truth and love. He brought faith, hope and love and embodied it."

~ *Pastor Mark D. Hornig, Mt. Olivet Lutheran Church, Sherwood Park, AB*

"Prophets must challenge evil, and not try to excuse conditions, times, current trends and what seems to be acceptable. We can be loving and kind by highlighting the effects of sin, the destruction physically and emotionally, etc. in this life and the eternal consequences in the next. Also, the challenge of pursuing real happiness of soul, mind, spirit, body – it is attainable."

~ John Forstner, Queen of Peace Roman Catholic prayer group, Saint John, NB

"The world cannot understand our message unless the Holy Spirit reveals it, but they can understand love and acts of caring. Our prophetic message must be seen as arising out of our own transformed hearts."

~ Anonymous

"To be honest in love, and loving in honesty, about what one is saying and believing and doing."

~ Keith Joyce, Christ Church Cathedral (Anglican), Fredericton, NB

"Raise up our youth – a prophetic generation."

~ Fr. Mark Cherry, St. Benedict Parish, Halifax, NS

"Incarnational – pastoral – relational. We speak the truth in love. The truth sets us free. If the truth is preached without love, it is not true. If we love without truth, it is not love. Our witness must be attractive and tasty (salty) for those yearning for God."

~ John Paul Westin, St. Thomas Anglican Church, St. John's, NL

"We Christians need to model authentically true Christian values personally, in our communities, business and churches. Not phony holiness – being vulnerable and honest."

~ Bob Baddeley, Ministry Director, Bethany Community Church, St. Catharines, ON

"Be prophetic to whom? Biblical prophets spoke to God's people – not to 'godless hordes.' The prophetic role of the Church does need to be a bit broader than our normal evangelical understandings. Are there justice issues we are overlooking? We need to be open to a larger evangelical consensus rather than to receive our prophetic marching orders 'from the top.'

This may keep us from courting and being co-opted by the 'powers.'"

~ Dr. Blayne Banting, Briercrest College and Seminary, Caronport, SK

"Different pastoral and doctrinal response: *Pastoral* – Love and care for all people, even 'enemies,' or those who have a different view than us. *Doctrinal* – God's truth cannot be compromised. There is a difference between acceptance and approval."

~ Rev. John Allsop, St. James United Church, Waterdown, ON

"Check our motives and listen to our critics and evaluate their message…. Create alternatives to issues we condemn. It is important to clearly articulate reasons for our prophetic voice, using the evidence available to us. There needs to be a prophetic voice in – and to – the Church first, before we take it public and expect unbelievers to respond. Make repentance as easy as possible. We need to model a balance to grace and truth."

~ Rick Wells, Lead Pastor of The Creek Community Church, Stoney Creek, ON

"The Church, united as a cross-denominational entity, should speak boldly against injustice and minister practically to relieve the suffering caused by injustice. If we focus too much on social justice without the balance of speaking anointed words to our culture, we fail to be the Church."

~ Stephen Whyte, Pastor of Paramount Drive Alliance Church, Stoney Creek, ON

"The ordinary Christian must set the balance by loving example…words into action. We must distinguish between tolerance and acceptance, and be clear in what we say. There are times to confront. We must judicially decide when it is time to confront."

~ Fr. Bob Bulbrook, St. Joseph's Parish, Acton, ON

"[We need] the light of Christ to shine through us…. We then are salty by the witness of Christ to the community at large."

~ Fr. Raymond Modeski, St. Patrick's Church, Burlington, ON

"The balance perhaps has been skewed. We have to restore balance and the role of the Church. When the purpose of an individual, church, or organization is unknown, the abuse of it is inevitable."

~ Pastor Daniel D. Saugh, Meadowvale Seventh Day Adventist Church, Mississauga, ON

"Pastors fail to point out this sin, likely due to: a) peer pressure, b) fear of being shunned because their position is contrary to the law of the land, c) speaking might alienate their membership, or d) some may seek personal comfort and acceptance, therefore, compromising themselves."

~ Rev. Suzanne Wilkinson, Chaplain, Toronto, ON

"This is certainly a tension that we struggle with. As salt, the Church does have a prophetic role in calling culture to a connection to God and realizing God's relationship with humanity and the earth. Balance is struck when we call the culture to its identity and relationship with God while embracing people with love, mercy, and acting justly toward them. We cross the line when we remain prophetic but do not embrace people at the same time. It was because of the embrace of people that the early Church won over an entire empire! *John 1* – Jesus came in grace and truth, and in that order. *Acts 2:42* – Jesus gained honour among people."

~ Luciano Lombardi, Master's College and Seminary, Toronto, ON

"The prophetic role is twofold: 1) social criticism and a call to social justice, 2) a call to return to a relationship with God. In short, to proclaim the summary of the law. It is not just a voice, it is healing action in society. And this voice and action come not from personal strength, but from being spirit-filled, in relationship with God, with Christ, and with the Holy Spirit."

~ Terry Wedge, Christ Church (Anglican), Brampton, ON

"The Church must be willing to spend money on kindness and acts of love to the needy. The Church earns its right to speak prophetically into the culture by being known for acts of love."

~ Lynda Tracy, First Hamilton Christian Reformed Church, Hamilton, ON

"Romans 12:21 says: *'Do not be overcome by evil, but overcome evil with good'* (NIV). We are too preoccupied with 'greatness' as a Church (growth, influence, successful programs) and we have let 'goodness' lapse."

~ Jim Klaas, Pastor of Discipleship, Kortright Presbyterian Church, Guelph, ON

"The prophetic role is to point people to God – to Christ. And not just the people outside the church walls, but to re-point, re-evangelize those pew-warmers. Define 'loving' and 'kind' in this day and age…. 'Love' in the culture is warm; fuzzy; I'm okay, you're okay. 'Loving' for Christians is to have a Christ-like love, being sacrificial – agape."

~ Rev. Kate McLarty, St. Alban's Anglican Church, Peterborough, ON

"We need to be good listeners to be able to share our views, while being open; not a judging ear to the voice of other views. We, as Christians, do not have the sole voice for Christ – He may just be speaking through the person seen as contrary to the Christian faith."

~ Fr. Paul Massel, St. Alphonsus Parish, Peterborough, ON

"The prophetic role of the Church must be solidly based on Scripture as its foundation. Scripture will balance justice and love."

~ Fr. Bernie Black, Assumption Roman Catholic Church, Hay River, NWT

Chapter 5

The Salt That Flavours

Governor Mike Huckabee, ordained minister and governor of Arkansas for more than 10 years, did not attend any of our pastors' meetings across Canada. But I would like to give him a voice in this book. I think we may agree (or maybe we won't!) that Huckabee is involved in a prophetic role; and that he, as of this writing, is succeeding fairly well at being loving and kind.

Huckabee came to be governor when the incumbent governor of his state was sentenced to prison. He joked that the five words most feared by Arkansas politicians are, "Will the defendant please rise." Huckabee has written, and shared quite openly, that he is a "conservative, pro-life, pro-family evangelical." He then gives us this explanation: "Despite partisan stereotypes, I'm not mad at everyone and my views are not driven by rage or even mild anger. The fact is, I'm a pretty happy guy most of the time. I have a simple philosophy – we need to take God more seriously and ourselves less seriously." I like that.

As a governor, moved by Christ's call to be loving and kind, Huckabee led the mobilization of his state to take in Katrina refugees from New Orleans. He was overjoyed by the response of the people in his state. Huckabee writes:

"The outpouring from the churches and faith-based groups was beyond anything we could have imagined. In fact, we simply had not anticipated the level of compassion that people would give. We had expected to need more state-provided staffing for the church camps who had agreed to feed and house people, and had underestimated that the church groups who operated the camps would have at their disposal thousands of ready, anxious, willing, and well-equipped volunteers who cancelled their Labour Day plans and left work in order to come and make beds, stir soup, organize recreational activities, sort and organize clothing, and provide loving care to their neighbours.... In the course of less than a week, an estimated 75,000 refugees poured into our state. That number increased our population by three percent."

For my home province of Ontario, on a per capita basis, this would mean mobilizing to care for an additional 450,000 people in a five-day period. Regardless of what happens to Rev. Huckabee's political future, he demonstrated in his state that a fervent Christian can distinguish himself as salt.

Salt in History

Jesus recognized three types amongst His followers: hot, cold or lukewarm. Every once in a while a hot ("cool" if you are under 40!) believer in Jesus as Saviour and Lord comes along who genuinely cares about the good of the people.

Sarah's Comments:

Have you heard of William Howland? He's the man who, more than any other, was responsible for "Toronto the Good." History calls him a "reform mayor." He served from 1886 to 1888, a time of rapid growth for Toronto. The following is my synopsis on William Howland's mayoral terms, based on the information I referenced from historian Desmond Morton, author of *Mayor Howland, a Citizen's Candidate.* I believe it demonstrates how a Christian can be salt in politics, for Howland has provided us an excellent example.

Transformation of a City

Immigration, natural growth, and the incorporation of neighbouring suburbs caused the city of Toronto to swell from 75,110 in 1880 to 104,276 in 1885. Although a prosperous community, it was also rife with problems. A major issue in the mid-1880s was the city's water supply. The drinking water was drawn from Lake

Ontario, but first had to pass through a series of rotten and leaking wooden pipes. The harbour, through which the pipes passed, was basically a giant sewage receptacle. Doctors were warning of a typhoid outbreak because of the water. However, for many citizens, this was not the worst of the city's problems. There were almost 300 legal taverns, plus countless other unlicensed drinking holes. More than half of the offences recorded in 1885 were directly related to drunkenness. The contemporary opinion was that strong drink lay at the root of almost all the social ills – from poverty to insanity.

The Toronto mayoral election of 1886 would be a historic one for the city: the first time Canadian women were allowed to vote. Even so, it was only unmarried women or widows who fulfilled the land ownership requirements that were able to vote. These voting women, however, would be strong supporters of Howland. Before the election of 1886, William Howland was known, not only for his political involvement in the city, but also for his philanthropy, religiosity and teetotalism. Howland did well as a businessman, making his fortune in the grain trade but by 1885 he was approaching bankruptcy.

Although William Howland grew up in the traditional church, the efforts of Dr. James Rainsford – an American evangelist who visited Toronto – brought him to a fervent evangelical faith. From that point on, he filled his time with good works at a considerable cost to his business. He was involved in the expansion of the Toronto General Hospital and the opening of coffeehouses to attract the working class away from the taverns. His evenings were devoted to charity work, like ministering to the needs of slum dwellers and prison inmates. He also launched the Christian Missionary Union in order to tend to those whose needs went beyond the provision of the local churches.

These experiences gave Howland empathy for the plight of Toronto's poor and, particularly, children. Delinquent youngsters and runaways were regularly thrown into the Don Jail, only to be preyed upon by older criminals. No other cause meant more to William Howland than collecting money and acquiring land to build a boys' industrial school.

Historians agree that Howland's status as a political independent was crucial to his 1886 mayoral victory. He ran on a platform of temperance, solving the city's water problem once and for all, tax cuts, and lowering the city debt. His victory on January 4th, 1886, was a sure one. As he began his term, Howland announced his program: to control liquor offences, he proposed that money from the fines be used to reward the informants; that second offenders be jailed for six months; and that the number of liquor licences be sharply reduced. Garbage disposal had become a nauseating problem and a threat to city health. To combat this problem, he proposed the construction of municipal furnaces. He also sought to improve the banks of the Don River, stating that this would attract manufacturers to the city. Under Howland's influence, a unit of mounted police was also recruited to patrol the suburbs.

Even though Howland was extremely busy with his duties as mayor, he still offered regular Bible classes and visited with the poor and vulnerable. Years before, at the General Hospital, he had witnessed a little boy being treated for broken limbs as a result of abuse. The incident only increased his fervour to care for abused women and children, appointing a special police officer to protect them. Even if siding with the poor meant not standing with the rich, Howland did not hesitate. During the infamous Street Railway strikes in Toronto, Howland supported the striking employees who had been forced to work endless hours for little pay.

Howland's support of their cause defined him as a mayor who truly cared about the working class citizens. He sought re-election in the 1887 election campaign, gaining a solid victory over his opponent. The 1887 term looked bright for Howland. Yet despite the sunny forecast of his political career, it proved to be a very difficult year. He was constantly met with bureaucracy on key issues; plus there were unsettling times in the city, thanks to a firebrand Irish political activist. Unfortunately, he was not able to rally enough support to implement further changes to the city's water supply, his budget was inadequate, and his own personal funds deteriorated as he continually put his finances into the mayoral duties. At the end of the 1887 term, Howland announced that he would not seek re-election – news that shocked and saddened his supporters.

Regardless of their disappointment, the Howland era had left its footprint on Canada's largest city. As a result, the city experienced great growth, both in numbers and infrastructure. However, it was not the material success that was most monumental; Toronto had come a long way in terms of morality and good government. Amazingly, the crime rate did not increase. In fact, the number of brothels and taverns actually went down. Historians agree that Howland's term boosted the morale of the city's working poor tremendously. Ironically, his own personal health and fortune deteriorated and, in 1893, he passed away at the age of 50. Author Desmond Morton reports that the city's poor loved Howland until the very end.

Part of Howland's success as mayor came because he placed his faith in God and the needs of others at the top of his priority list. When most people would have caved in under the institutional pressure to serve the wealthy and influential, Howland did not balk. It was precisely this fortitude that allowed him to make such positive changes for Toronto, and take steps to care for the downtrodden of the city. In a day and age when the least influential members of society are often forgotten, we would all do well to learn from William Howland's example. He was truly a salty Christian.

A Mother's Love Touches the World

Another salty Christian you are probably more familiar with is, of course, Mother Teresa. She was salt. How did a diminutive Albanian woman, working in far-off Calcutta, India, exercise her strong prophetic voice? One very public time occurred at Harvard University, where Mother Teresa spoke to America's future elites and received the longest standing ovation in the history of that institution. In her talk, she encouraged chastity and condemned abortion. Later, in an interview with *TIME* magazine, the interviewer asked about her strength to raise such difficult issues. Mother Teresa replied, "We must tell the truth."

Mother Teresa's Harvard audience could hear her – and still respect her – because of her work for the poor. Even that secular gathering knew salt when they tasted it. Mother Teresa died at Calcutta's Mission of Mercy Hospital, a healthcare institution founded by two salty Canadian Christians, Mark and Huldah Buntain.

Chapter 6

Being the Church – and Salt – in a World of Politics

Sarah's Comments:

The Church must have some kind of role in the political process, but what is that role, and when and where do we cross the line? These are important questions as Christians work out how best to interact in the political public square.

Some Christians believe that Canada is a Christian country, founded on Christian principles; therefore, our government should be a Christian government, founded on traditional Biblical values. Canada may have been founded on Christian principles, but can we call Canada a Christian country today? What actually defines a Christian country?

I prefer to call Canada a country with Christians in it. We must make an honest appraisal about what is realistic in politics. For example, many Christians believe abortion is morally wrong. I am one of them. But to expect a political leader to abolish abortion, which has been widely accepted and practised for many years (therapeutically, since 1969, and on demand since 1988), is unrealistic. We must understand that change is made in small steps. In politics, Christians must accept the controversial fact that sometimes there is a gray area; not every issue has to be black and white. To withdraw support from a government leader for failing to live up the notion of a Christian society is unrealistic.

We are a minority. Yet we often expect the government should be run exactly to our standards. But that would not fairly represent the people of Canada and would fail as a democracy. The government will most often reflect how Canada is at any given point in history. We need to accept that with grace, while not resigning our vigilant posts and just letting things be. And we *should* carefully articulate Biblical values to government leaders. However, it is unfair to expect that a nation made up of so many diverse peoples is going to be exactly the way a minority of people expect that it should be.

Some Christians tend to flock to certain issues and neglect others that are just as important. The "moral" issues get championed by the Church and Christians, issues such as abortion, the marriage debate and euthanasia. But what about the other moral issues like justice, equality, human rights, fair wages, and environmental concerns? How about more of a helping hand to those living below the poverty line or in other oppressive circumstances? What about Aboriginal issues? Poverty in the developing world?

These Christians have, to their detriment, focussed so much on certain "hot button" issues and let others slide. The Church could work harder to have a well-rounded approach to politics, rather than focussing all our attentions only on certain issues. These hot-button issues should not be ignored, but prioritized.

We, as the Church, certainly do have a right to be involved in politics, and should have a voice in society. In the ideal world, our voice would be a unified voice on all fronts, standing up for truth; a truth that seeks justice and righteousness. The voice of truth does not neglect issues that are of equal importance. I believe that we vastly underestimate the influence that we as Christians could have on our country.

So what are the rights and responsibilities of the Church in politics? This is not a definitive list, and it is shaped by what we learned speaking with Christian leaders across Canada.

1. **We have the responsibility to pray for our country, and our leaders**.
   Prayer changes things. We have the right and privilege to pray for our country, our leaders, those with whom we agree, and those with whom we do not agree. It's not a revolutionary concept, but it can have a revolutionary impact.

2. **We have the responsibility to enable and encourage congregation members to vote.**
   It is important that all of us, including clergy, encourage

congregants to get out and vote. For those reluctant to partake in politics, this means encouraging and persuading members to participate. This may mean practical acts like driving congregants to polling stations for those who cannot get out to vote.

3. **We have the right to vote according to our conscience.**
   It is not a good idea for a specific political party to be promoted from the pulpit. The idea that there is one party that is more Christian than another is erroneous and has caused confusion.

4. **We have a responsibility to stand up for what we believe.**
   The Church (comprised of individual Christians), must articulate to the government its views and values. We must be confident that we have much to offer society that would improve the quality of life on a wide range of issues.

5. **We have the right to live free of stereotype.**
   Christians do not all agree on politics. Too often Christians have had the labels of "ultra-conservative" or "fundamentalist" applied to them. There is no one "Christian" political party. Within each party, there are Christian members. We have the right not to be labelled in a stereotypical way.

6. **We have the right to have our Christian faith recognized, respected and not belittled.**
   Christianity has a long history in Canada. Many former leaders who have shaped and defined Canada have confessed a faith in Christ. As former Prime Minister Pierre Trudeau stated on *100 Huntley Street*: "The golden thread of faith is woven throughout the history of Canada from its earliest beginnings up to the present time. Faith

was more important than commerce in the minds of many of the European explorers and settlers." Many freedoms that we now enjoy in Canada were directly related to members of the faith community who fought for these freedoms.

Rising to Meet the Salt Challenge

Our society is becoming increasingly secular. In a society that is against much of what we profess as Christians, how can we be productive members? We don't have to blend into our surroundings. Sometimes what the world needs is a refreshingly different perspective. I have found that people I talk to about some of my more "conservative" views are often surprisingly receptive.

What are Christian values? For many this means The Ten Commandments, The Golden Rule, and the sanctity of marriage. I would not call these things Canadian values. And they are not American values, or British, or Scandinavian, or of any other country. They are Christian human values. Of course, Canadian values will change over the years because Canadians are changing. Death, birth, immigration – our country is constantly in motion with change. The value system of the country will continue to be fluid. This is not a destruction of the historical Christian traditions. It is a natural phenomena occurring with the changing tide. And we can rise to meet its challenges.

David's Comments:

In 1981, something called *Salute to Canada* crossed our nation. It was essentially a prayer pilgrimage across Canada. The first event was on the west coast in Victoria, British Columbia. Here's what happened early that first morning, as I reported in my book, *God Keep Our Land.*

"I knew I should be getting some rest, but sleep was impossible. If I went to bed now, I would just lie awake, staring at the ceiling. 'Norma-Jean, I'm going for a walk,' I announced, exiting the motel room before my wife could reply.

"It was June 1st, and outside, the gathering dusk was warm and fragrant. Victoria, the crown jewel of British Columbia, was world-famous for its gardens, and there was a freshness in the evening air that indicated summer would soon be more than just a promise.

"I strolled over to the Legislative Building that marked the seat of the provincial capital. This magnificent gothic-style stone structure, erected at the end of the last century [referring to the 19th century], when the sun was still at high noon over the British Empire, was outlined at night by thousands of light bulbs, dramatically enhancing its presence. Often before, while visiting Victoria, I marvelled at the splendour of this sight, and I'd always had a hankering to be standing right in front, when the lights went on. This evening, it looked like I had arrived in time.

"As I gazed at the edifice, I was startled by a voice at my elbow. 'You an admirer of architecture?' 'Not particularly,' I replied, adding a smile, so as not to hurt the feelings of the little old lady who stood next to me. She must have been at least 80, and she was bundled up and leaning on a cane. 'I've been bed-ridden for most of the past year,' she volunteered, when no further comment was forthcoming from me. None was needed, it seemed. She went right on, pleased to have someone to share her good news with. 'This is the first time I've been able to come out for a walk.'

"Raising her cane, she pointed with it at a temporary speaker's platform which extended out from the wide stone front steps that led up to the building's main entrance. 'That means they've either just had some do, or are about to have one,' she informed me, with the uninhibited frankness of an octogenarian who had long ago ceased caring about what others thought of her. I nodded as if I already knew, and she cocked an eye up at me, suddenly suspicious. 'What do you do?'

"I went on to explain to the woman that I was a preacher, and that the platform was to launch a month-long *Salute to Canada,* with live telecasts in 25 cities from coast to coast. The lady said that she had never heard of me and that she didn't watch much television. At that moment, the lights turned on and the legislative building glowed. It was beautiful, like something out of a fairy tale. Then, my new friend asked me: 'Why are you doing this – um, whatever you called it?' 'The Salute?' I answered. 'Well, our purpose is to unite the nation in prayer and to call on Canadian Christians to repent that God might heal our land. We're starting here tomorrow, and we're ending on July 1ˢᵗ, Canada's birthday, in Charlottetown, Prince Edward Island, where it all began.

"She seemed singularly unimpressed. Looking up at me and frowning, she wagged her finger under my nose. 'I'm an Anglican, though it's been a long time since I've been able to get to church. But let me tell you something,' and she paused to let the full weight of her fourscore years underline what she was about to say. 'Don't waste time on pomp and ceremony. You said you were coming to pray, then concentrate on the business of praying!' I thanked my new friend and, in my heart, I thanked God. I decided to do what His outspoken messenger had told me to do."

Prayer is indeed the highest right and greatest responsibility of the Church. Paul said it best: *"Therefore I exhort **first of all** that supplications, prayers, intercessions and giving of thanks be made for all men, for kings and all who are in authority, that we may lead a quiet and peaceable life in all godliness and reverence. For this is good and acceptable in the sight of God our Saviour, who desires all men to be saved and to come to the knowledge of the truth"* (1 Timothy 2:1-4).

Back in 1981, I learned some important lessons. I believe that our *Salute to Canada* was apolitical. Even so, some of the secular media were already trying to equate it with the Moral Majority movement in the States. But nothing could have been further from the truth. The last thing we wanted was to insert ourselves into the fabric of Canadian society as a political force in any manner.

We were, in spirit, much closer to the heart of *Washington For Jesus,* which had seen nearly half a million Americans gather in their nation's capital the year before to pray for their country, and to repent – not for what their politicians or their fellow countrymen had been doing, but for their *own* sins. They weren't pointing a finger or trying to lobby; they were humbling themselves.

Our *Salute to Canada* had already been in the works for several months when we sent a group from *100 Huntley Street* to join the *Washington for Jesus* contingent in the march down Constitution Avenue. Our people reported back that there was no contention or denunciation; there was, instead, peace and humility and joy. And that was what I had intended the *Salute to Canada* to reflect.

One of our guests that afternoon was Grace McCarthy, deputy premier of British Columbia, who thanked all Canadians for their prayers and then reminded them of how fortunate they were: "We need to be thankful for the right of free assembly, which is being demonstrated here today. Many nations do not have that. We should be thankful for the freedom to worship as we choose. Many nations do not have that either. In fact, there are untold millions who would give anything to trade places with the poorest Canadian in this land." She closed by underlining the new phrase in our national anthem, which summed up the whole purpose of our prayer pilgrimage: "God keep our land." After that, not surprisingly, we sang *O Canada* and, as we did, I found my eye drawn to that huge maple leaf on the flag overhead.

"You know," I said to the people, when we had finished singing, "Ours is the only flag in the world with a single leaf on it. And there's a verse in Scripture which talks about a tree of life, the leaves of which would be for the healing of the nations. I believe that this may well be Canada's role: To serve the rest of the world in prayer. When Billy Graham was on *100 Huntley Street* a while back, he said that Canada may never be a military superpower, or an economic superpower, but she could become a spiritual superpower, showing the rest of the world the way. And when he said that, a number of us

had that spine-tingling feeling that he was speaking prophetically."
I paused and looked at them. "Was he? It's up to us, you know –
you and me, standing here." And it is still up to us – you and me,
standing here in this place, in this time... being salt.

Speaking of Salt

If you stop and think about it, we all have great stories of salt
and how it impacts the world, just as Jesus said it would. Here's
another one. It happened in March of 1978. My wife Norma-Jean
and I had taken our two boys to the Holy Land for a backpacking
expedition (actually, the boys and I hiked, and their mother followed
in a borrowed Volkswagen™). We happened to be in Jerusalem
when former U.S. President Jimmy Carter flew to Israel to make his
historical appeal before the Knesset, as a last-ditch, personal effort to
salvage whatever might be left of the Camp David Peace Accords.

The general consensus among political observers inferred that
he was wasting his time; the accords were being written off as
defunct, as was any real chance for a lasting peace agreement. And
so I prayed, hardly knowing exactly how to pray, except that I felt
a little like what a woman must feel in labour. I prayed for three
hours. It was what the old Methodists used to call "praying through"
and, at the end of that time, I had the sense that victory in the
spirit realm had been won. And soon after, the peace accords were
announced. There's an old saying, that when someone undertakes a
heavy intercessory burden, they should not be surprised if they're
somehow involved in God's solution.

During Carter's mission, I applied for a press pass. Before I
knew it, I was a fully accredited member of the press corps covering
the president's visit, and I dutifully phoned in daily reports to *100
Huntley Street,* coordinating the seven-hour time differential so they
could be carried live. By Monday, the final day, so many media
people had converged on Jerusalem from all over the world that
they had to move press headquarters to the Jerusalem Theatre to
accommodate all 800 of us.

The reception of the president in the Knesset was chilly, to
put it mildly. And when he insisted in his speech that the people

wanted peace, the Israeli legislators took it that he was implying that the leadership themselves, did not. He finished to a spattering of applause. The general response among the press corps was that Carter had been foolish to come to the Middle East himself, and that he had sacrificed the last vestiges of whatever remaining international stature he may have had.

Carter himself was livid (I learned later from his sister Ruth), and was determined never to speak to Begin again and just go home, take his lumps and try to forget the whole thing. Word came through that he had left the Knesset and was going to visit the Shrine of the Book, where the Dead Sea Scrolls were kept. There, he would pass enough time for them to establish the necessary security precautions to guard his departure on Air Force One, which was waiting in Tel Aviv.

Meanwhile, in the theatre, everything was winding down. Reporters were queuing up and getting into the press buses that would take them to the airport in time for the president's departure, to be followed as quickly as possibly by their own.

It had been a real downer of an assignment, and the journalists were anxious to return home and get to work on something more upbeat. The theatre was almost empty, when two radio newscasters – one of them from the local Hebrew station and the other from the local Arabic station – looked at one another, shrugged in my direction and then came over and asked, "Would you mind if we interviewed you about the Carter mission? They would immediately translate it into Hebrew and Arabic, and put it out live over both stations."

I blinked. "Are you sure you've got the right person? I'm a preacher from Canada." They looked at each other, making no attempt to mask their boredom and fatigue, and again shrugged. "You'll do," one said. We sat down and they posed the question which they must have asked dozens of more qualified commentators over the past 72 hours: "Do you think there's any chance for peace?"

While I wondered what to say, I felt my scalp tighten, and the Spirit of God came over me like He never had before. I felt utterly immobilized in the clamp of God, powerless to do or say anything but that which He specifically gave me to say. The thought fleeted across my mind that this must have been what the Old Testament prophets felt like. And it occurred to me, at that very moment, literally millions of Jews and Arabs were listening to their radios at home, at work, in the car, and on bicycles, because their future – and possibly their lives – depended upon the outcome of that day's events.

Into my heart came the words that God wanted me to speak, and I started to tremble, because they seemed impossible – exactly counter to what the most astute political observers had been saying, even before Carter had left the Knesset in disgust. But I had no choice. I opened my mouth and the words came out: "There shall be a miraculous breakthrough, by the God of Abraham, Isaac and Jacob!"

The two reporters were stunned by this, but no more so than me. I went on, and they went on translating. "Never before in history, have three great leaders of three different religions prayed for peace to the same God. And He is the same, regardless by what name they call Him. In fact, last night I heard Prime Minister Begin quote the hymn, 'I truly believe in the coming of the Messiah.' I believe in that too and, while the Messiah waits, He is answering the prayers of millions of people for the peace of Jerusalem on this occasion."

I paused, and God's grip tightened. "Peace is His will. It is His plan. There shall be a miraculous breakthrough!" With that, the interview concluded. I hurried to the phone bank and called home. It was two in the afternoon in Jerusalem, which made it seven in the morning at *100 Huntley Street.* They taped my report for airing on the morning's show which went to air at least two hours before the first excited secular news bulletin that something miraculous did indeed appear to be happening: the president's plane was being returned to its hangar! The successful implementation of the Camp David Peace Accords followed.

Years later, in Kitchener, Ontario, I was with President Carter in a Habitat for Humanity building project. With my weakness for tears very obvious, I told him the story. The intensely cerebral Carter patted me on the back and said, "There, there." I'm not sure he fully believed me, but at least he was moved by my tears.

Nothing like that had ever happened to me before and it has not happened to me since. I dare not expect such an experience again. But may the Church always remember that God reserves the right to intervene in human history any time He pleases. The gifts of the

Spirit, such as the word of wisdom and the word of knowledge, are still given to the Church. *"But one and the same Spirit works all these things, distributing to each one individually as He wills"* (1 Corinthians 12:11). Don't underestimate the Holy Spirit. He may surprise each reader at some point in life. There are Biblical precedents, not only in the prophets, but in the predictions of Jesus regarding the Temple and to the Apostle Paul on board the Roman prison ship. It seems apparent that even the political complexion of Rome was altered. Paul could write, *"All the saints greet you, but especially those who are of Caesar's household"* (Philippians 4:22). Likewise, President Carter, a confessed born-again political leader was salt indeed.

Here are some more answers and insights from Christian leaders from across Canada, answering a very difficult and potentially explosive question. I think you will find their responses interesting and challenging. As you read, consider what your answer to this question might be:

3. As it is believed best for the Church not to endorse specific political parties or candidates, please respond to this question: What are the rights and responsibilities of the Church in the political process?

"Invite candidates to speak and be asked questions by church members. Christians as individuals or groups – not necessarily as a Church – may lobby political leaders. For the Church to attain influence and be prophetic so that government listens to it may be dangerous. The job of the Church is to proclaim the Gospel in every segment of the society."
~ Ernie Pinzon, Filipino Community Church, Ottawa, ON

"The Church needs to fortify its members to live by core Biblical principles and challenge them to participate in the political life of their nation. I am not comfortable with the Church endorsing particular parties, because this could bring problems for the Church, especially if the government fails at any point."
~ Anonymous

"I believe in the separation of Church and state, but I also believe it is incumbent upon Christians to become well-informed as to what political parties and their individual members stand for, and vote accordingly."

~ Rev. Bill Bresnahan, Grace United Church, Gananoque, ON

"Encourage participation at a grassroots level (individuals), and have a truth focus (values, morality) that transcends a political party. Hold them all accountable to truth. We are responsible to model a better way by having great marriages, being great neighbours, and by supporting justice. Produce great literature, music and art that is wholesome. Help the family thrive and teach Christian marriage."

~ Pastor Ted Boodle, West Winds Community Church, Surrey, BC

"Be a voice, encourage people to vote, make phone calls and get involved. In our fear of being politically correct, we have remained silent and now our country bears the burden of this silence. Educate the Body of our responsibility to speak out. God has granted us the privilege to live here.... On moral and ethical issues, taking a strong Biblical stand is essential. It is our responsibility to speak about these things. We have a responsibility to teach a Biblical worldview and continue to address current social issues in light of Holy Scripture."

~ Norah Kennedy, Director of Pregnancy Care Centre, Edmonton, AB

"The Church should be the foundational structure of any political regime. The Church and government should partner together like a husband and wife, both fulfilling separate but equally important roles. Jesus was with the people. He never held himself aloof."

~ Karen Hardy, Saint John Community Chaplaincy, Saint John, NB

"...To care for the politician as well as the politics."

~ Keith Joyce, Christ Church Cathedral (Anglican), Fredericton, NB

"...To commission our laity to be salt and light, to rediscover a sense of apostolate, to 'send' our people. We have substituted an 'ad intra' sense of ministry, for a missionary 'apostolate.' Lay people should be formed and sent into the world of media and politics."

~ Fr. James Mallon, St. Thomas Aquinas Canadian Martyrs, Halifax, NS

"The Christian politician needs to deal with the tension of serving God and the constituency. The 'rights' terminology may point the question in the wrong direction – a more secular understanding rather than Biblical one. We need to recognize our responsibility to uphold truth wherever it is found and, likewise, to stand against wrong, even when perpetrated by 'our' party or candidate. We need to guard against the naive view that, if we could only get enough Christians in government, we will have a Christian country. Jesus is coming back but Constantine is not!"

~ Dr. Blayne Banting, Briercrest College and Seminary, Caronport, SK

"...Key word: 'How TRUSTWORTHY are we as Christians?' Can we expect a politician to be trustworthy when the Christian community is fragmented by internal fighting, bickering, and backbiting?"

~ John Adams, Counsellor at The Caring Place Christian Counselling Centre, Regina, SK

"Declaration with demonstration, as Jesus practised what He preached. He didn't take on political issues but He dealt with the fallout. Jesus confronted 'untruths' and went public with the message. Are we willing to die for our faith like Jesus did? Jesus talked to people about the Kingdom of God."

~ Chris Orford, Harvest Bible Chapel, Oakville, ON

"When you vote, you don't vote for the Kingdom of God. Help identify and draw attention to the issues and encourage people to think creatively about these issues."

~ Rev. John Allsop, St. James United, Waterdown, ON

"Jesus did not engage the political system, but effected political fallout and change."

~ Rev. Ray David Glenn, St. George's Anglican Church, Lowville, ON

"Establish relationships with present leaders, encouraging them to make choices that honour human beings. Gain a voice and be heard by establishing friendships and honouring them as human beings."

~ Luciano Lombardi, Master's College and Seminary, Toronto, ON

"The rights and responsibilities of churches are to be a clear voice of objective truth (who is Jesus) to society and to be fully engaged in culture."

~ Fr. Graham Keep, Mary Immaculate Parish, London, ON

"We, the Church, must stay strong in what the Bible says. There is too much emphasis on human rights. The emphasis must be on God's rights and His Word. We must follow God's laws first and, secondly, the laws of the land and government."

~ Chief Alec Sunrise, Hay River First Nation, NWT

"The rights and responsibilities of churches are to be a clear voice of objective truth (who is Jesus) to society and to be fully engaged in culture."

~ Fr. Graham Keep

Chapter 7

The Preserving Power of Salt

I was ordained in 1959. I love the Church. She is the Bride of Christ. He loves her and He gave Himself for her. But is the Church perfect? It could not be, because I'm a member. We are the only organism ordered by the Founder to love and receive *all* people – that means bad and good, crooked and straight. Over the past years, I've often been asked, "And what do you do?" I usually mumble something unintelligible and try to change the subject. I would like to move the conversation to a witness for Jesus. I don't want to talk about TV evangelists. Can I get any sympathy on that?

I am convinced that, while we may use the mass media to call for decisions for Christ as Billy Graham does (and I thank God that I can talk about Billy as part of my witness for Christ), it is the neighbour or the person at work or school who can be the most effective witness. All the members, along with their pastors, are the very best people to share their faith.

My grandson, David-Peter Mainse (Reynold and Kathy's son), did just that in the year 2002. This article from *The Hamilton Spectator* tells how.

Street Sleep 'Remarkable' Fundraiser
Eight-year-old raises $3,372.93 for homeless

By Sylvia Gudzowski
Special to *The Hamilton Spectator*

His father says that on the outside, he looks like any typical, rugged eight-year-old. But David-Peter Mainse proved that, on the inside, he is a kid with an extraordinary love for people. The evidence was a cheque worth

---

$3,372.93 which he handed over to three local organizations that help Hamilton's homeless.

The money was raised to support One Homeless Night, a family awareness campaign inspired by Mainse's curiosity about what it would feel like to be homeless. He wanted to get a better understanding of life without the basic necessities, and he wanted to do something to help. So his parents, Reynold

David-Peter Mainse, 8, sits on the piece of cardboard he slept on overnight and smiles while talking about friends who emptied piggy banks to help the homeless.

and Kathy Mainse, who work for Crossroads Christian Communications Inc. in Burlington, felt the best way to satisfy his curiosity was to let him experience it first hand.

On October 13, after a week of donation and pledge-seeking, the Mainse family left the warmth of their Ancaster home and stepped into the cold reality of Hamilton's streets. "I have a seven-year-old boy, and he is into his Game Boy, his computer and the television. Most kids at that age are self-absorbed," said Alan Craig of The Living Rock, a resource centre for street youth. The money raised will be split between The Living Rock, Mission Services and 96 James Street Inc. "For a kid like David-Peter to break away from that and get a vision beyond himself is remarkable," said Craig.

The family spent their homeless night visiting shelters, talking with people and listening to their stories before making their way to the cardboard boxes in front of James Street Baptist Church where they slept. David-Peter remembers the night as long and cold – a definite eye-opener. "I learned not to be picky or selfish," said the third-grade Grange Elementary student, grandson of *100 Huntley Street* host Rev. David Mainse. "There are lots of people out there who don't have anything to eat or any stuff to keep them warm. And we have everything."

He is happy with the community response and he smiles ear-to-ear when talking about the support of friends. "They emptied out their piggy banks and gave all the money to me," he said. "I think that was really nice of them."

Pastor Don Berry-Graham, of James Street Baptist Church, said David-Peter may have inspired plans to get others in the community to experience life on the streets first hand. "We might want to get some families or individuals to raise money and have One Homeless Night," he said. "Or we could get the president of Stelco to come down for a night on the streets – just as a way to raise money and find out what it's like to live on the streets."

Ward 2 Councillor Andrea Horwath thanked David-Peter on behalf of the city for helping raise awareness of the often overlooked homeless situation. "It's amazing that such a young person can make that connection, and realize that it's not just a number, it's a reality of actual people who have had various life circumstances," she said. "It's a very courageous thing to do to walk in the sandals of another human being. And it's especially heartening to see that this was mostly about how to help."

Although he is not yet quite sure how, David-Peter is definitely willing to do more to help. "If I could, I would do it again," he said.

David-Peter's act was a prophetic one. He made his parents, and even his Grandpa, look good. And as a by-product, the Church looked good. That's salt.

The Hamilton International Airport was named after the late Hon. John Munroe. John had been a minister of the Crown for many years as Minister of Labour, Minister of Aboriginal Affairs and Minister of Health. He also got up at 2:30 in the morning and travelled to the downtown Hamilton street corner where my grandson and his family were trying to sleep on their cardboards to encourage them. That's salt.

We must confess that throughout history, when the Church has ruled in civil government, we have not always done well, but the Church can bless, inspire, and sometimes correct and persuade with great effect. That's being salty.

This prophetic role must be undergirded by credibility and modesty in lifestyle and faithfulness to vows like marriage, children and ordination. It is marked by interdependence with others in the Church, not burning bridges in relationships. It is marked by no offense and no defence on the human level. Its hallmark is transparency in finances and in our failings.

The writings of St. Paul, the former Saul of Tarsus, work hand-in-hand with the salt sermon of Jesus. Paul actually "got" it. He understood what it meant to be salt. I've just completed the spiritual exercise of reading with very few breaks all of his New Testament writings. I encourage you to do the same.

Paul writes, *"Now the purpose of the commandment is love from a pure heart, from a good conscience, and from sincere faith from which some have strayed having turned aside to idle talk, desiring to be teachers of the law, understanding neither what they say nor the things which they affirm"* (1 Timothy 1:5-7). Verse 12 is my ordination word: *"I thank Christ Jesus our Lord who has enabled me, because He counted me faithful, putting me into the ministry."* At difficult times, and there have been many, I've comforted myself with those words. The writings of Paul taste quite salty to me, I'm sure they will to you as well.

The Building Blocks of Ministry

A book I treasure was given to me by my father, Rev. Dr. Roy Lake Mainse. It is called *The Holiness Movement Discipline*. My father came from Methodist roots and loved to quote its founder, Rev. John Wesley, who exercised a powerful apostolic ministry. My grandparents became deeply committed to the Holiness Movement, a Methodist revival of Wesley's teachings and writings about his personal experience with Christ. Churches such as the Wesleyan Methodist Church, the Salvation Army, the Free Methodist Church, the Nazarene Church, and others arose to preach and serve.

I think you may agree that before a prophetic impact on our social and moral order can be effective, the one who speaks in the name of Christ must be a partaker in the life of Christ. Biblically, the priest represents man to God, and the prophet represents God to man. Jesus Himself exercised both of these offices.

The book my father gave me is old. It represents the vows of ordination that Christian leaders embraced 100 years ago. The words represent a very high calling. It is a calling that we modern

Christian leaders are living out today. These phrases help provide some of the building blocks of salt that we need as priests, ministers and clergy of all types. As you read these ancient-sounding words, contemplate how they fit with your view of your own ministry; and how, if followed, they could increase your salt witness to your family, your congregation, and to your world.

On "The Ministry"
(From *The Holiness Movement Discipline*)

Those who profess to be called of God to the ministry should be recommended to the annual conference by a society or by a member of conference. The following or other similar questions shall be asked concerning them:

- Do they know God as a pardoning God?
- Have they the love of God abiding in them?
- Do they desire nothing but God?
- Are they holy in all manner of conversation?
- Have they, in some tolerable degree, a clear, sound understanding, a right judgment in the things of God, a just conception of salvation by faith?
- Has God given them any degree of utterance?
- Do they speak justly, readily, clearly?
- Have they fruit?
- Are any truly convinced of sin and converted to God by their preaching?

As long as these marks concur in anyone, we believe he is called of God to preach. These we receive as sufficient proof that he is moved by the Holy Ghost. They shall then be called before the conference and be required to give satisfactory answers to the following questions:

- Have you faith in Christ?
- Have you the Enduement of Power from on High?

- Will you endeavour not to speak too long or too loud?
- Will you diligently instruct the children in every place?
- Will you visit from house to house?

This next section considers the commitments that those called to ministry make to their own spiritual lives. I know how incredibly busy your lives can be as Christian leaders. It can be non-stop. Ministry, as full of rewards as it is, can be relentless. The famous theologian, J.I. Packer, quoted these practical words of wisdom in an interview recently with the Canadian *Faith Today* magazine:

"When you are in the ministry, you must take charge of your own time, your own program. You must discipline yourself. You should make yourself a timetable for the working week and try to stick to it. There are two reasons for that. First, nobody is going to supervise you very carefully. If you allow yourself to be lazy and undisciplined, no one might notice. And the second is that undiscipline, laziness and disorder are, from Satan's point of view, virtues he values. After 20 years of not achieving very much, the minister will have a nervous breakdown, burn out, and so on, and have to be laid off work. It's inner disorder that produces these burnouts and breakdowns most of the time. People who work very hard but have taken charge of their own lives – and their lives are orderly – don't have burnouts."

Consider what ministers pledged to do 100 years ago to avoid that kind of burnout, once again, reviewing a section from *The Holiness Movement Discipline.*

The Duty of Preachers to God, Themselves and to One Another

Question: **How shall the preacher be qualified for his charge?**
Answer: *By walking closely with God and having his work greatly at heart; and by understanding, and loving discipline.*

Question: **Do we watch sufficiently over each other?**
Answer: *We do not. Should we not frequently ask each other, do you walk closely with God? Have you now fellowship with the Father and Son? At what hour do you rise? Do you punctually observe the morning and evening hour of retirement? Do you spend the day in the manner which the conference advises? Do you converse seriously, usefully and closely?*

The instituted are:

I. *Prayer* - Private, family and public; consisting of deprecation, petition, intercession and thanksgiving.
Do you use each of these? Do you forecast daily wherever you are, to secure time for private devotion? Do you practise it everywhere? Do you ask everywhere, "Have you family prayer?" Do you ask individuals, "Do you use private prayer every morning and evening in particular?"

II. *Searching the Scriptures by:*
(1) Reading constantly some part, every day regularly, all the Bible in order; carefully with notes; seriously, with prayer before and after; fruitfully, immediately practising what you learn there.
(2) Meditating at set times. By rule.
(3) Hearing: Every opportunity. With prayer before and after. Have you a Bible always about you?

III. *The Lord's Supper*
Do you use this at every opportunity; with solemn prayer before? With earnest and deliberate self-devotion?

IV. *Fasting* - Do you use as much abstinence and fasting every week, as your health, strength, and labour will permit?

V. *Christian Conversation* - Are you convinced how important and how difficult it is to order your conversation aright? Is it always in grace? Seasoned with salt? Meet to minister grace to the hearers? Do you not converse too long at a time? Is not an hour commonly long enough? Would it not be well always to have a determinate end in view? And to pray before and after it?

VI. *Prudential Means* we may use, either as Christians or as preachers.

(1) As Christians: What particular rules have you in order to grow in grace? What arts of holy living?

(2) As preachers: Have you thoroughly considered your duty? And do you make a conscience of executing every part of it? Do you meet every society?

These means may be used without fruit. But there are some means which cannot; namely, watching, denying ourselves, taking up our cross, exercising the presence of God.

1. Do you steadily watch against the world? Yourself? Your besetting sin?
2. Do you deny yourself every useless pleasure of sense? Imagination? Honour? Are you temperate in all things?
   (1) Do you use only that kind and that degree which is best both for body and soul? Do you see the necessity in this?
   (2) Do you eat no more at each meal than is necessary? Are you not heavy or drowsy after dinner?
   (3) Do you use only that kind and that degree of drink which is best both for your body and soul?
   (4) Do you choose and use water for your common drink? And only take wine medicinally or sacramentally?
3. Wherein do you take up your cross daily? Do you cheerfully bear your cross, however grievous, to profit thereby?
4. Do you endeavour to set God always before you? To see His eye continually fixed upon you? Never can you use

these means but a blessing will ensue, and the more you use them, the more you will grow in grace.

I've quoted extensively from the book my father gave me. In presenting it to me, he gave me a way of life; an order to ministry that has helped keep my path narrow and salty.

The Scriptures tell us, *"Know thyself."* I most certainly have not always done what I should have done, and I have not always been what I should have been. I've sincerely asked God to grant me the grace of living in a constant attitude of repentance. Even St. Paul wrote, *"...what I want to do, I do not do..."* (Romans 7:15 NIV). We've all seen sculptures of great men and women of God. They look so perfect but, remember, the statues are not human.

Humans fail, but the believer is *"in Christ"* and *"Jesus never fails."* We can, we must, and we will do as Paul declared, *"I press toward the mark for the prize of the high calling of God in Christ Jesus"* (Philippians 3:14 KJV).

I'm convinced that the degree to which we exercise a prophetic role effectively is directly in proportion to the degree in which we follow Christ. The next question we asked our clergy participants has to do with moral and social decay, and what the Church can do about it. Sarah, as a younger voice, will offer her perspective first.

Sarah's Comments:

We are living in a time where institutions are becoming increasingly mistrusted and suspect – and with good reason. People are realizing that there are no perfect institutions, and religious organizations seem to be at the top of that list. There is also a pervading idea that institutions care only for themselves and not for individuals. They are impersonal. They are cold. They are filled with bureaucracy. There is always media coverage eager to show the fall of another "man of God" – and it seems to happen often.

Many baby boomer Canadians were raised going to church, or at least with some kind of church exposure in their lives. Subsequent generations are becoming more and more Biblically illiterate. Instead of pointing the finger, let's consider if we may have contributed to the problem. Did the Church in the past offer an accurate picture of Christ to the people? Did we offer the kind of faith that people would want to live out and pass on to their children? Much of a person's spiritual journey is a personal, self-initiated decision. I don't think a church will ever succeed in introducing God to someone who doesn't want to find Him (or be found by Him). The Church can paint a picture of Christ which is so accurate that it attracts people, and by simply living the lifestyle of following Christ. The lifestyle of Christ was radically others-centred and radically giving. It is precisely this lifestyle, lived out by His devoted followers, that is the most powerful witness.

People have always been searching for God, and many have concluded that He cannot be found inside a church. People want something real so desperately. Are we giving them something real? Are we being transparent? Christians can be incredibly preoccupied with hiding personal flaws. Our Christian culture gives us another reason to put on a mask, or we may not fit in with all the other Christians wearing their masks.

I believe the shortcomings of the Church in the past are being felt in this generation of youth and young adults. Maybe the fact that Canada has a tradition of Christianity is part of our problem in reaching people for Christ. Hundreds of years of accepted traditions and very little outside challenge has created a state of complacency that is killing the Church.

But I see something happening, at least within my framework. I see a desire to strip away phony appearances and be real. People yearn to say, "Yes, I am a Christian and I have committed my life to Christ – but let's be real. Let's face up to the issues we have as the faith community and as human beings, and let's reach out to our neighbours, our country, and our world."

According to the census, the Church has been in a slow and steady decline for decades. There aren't enough young people coming in to replace the aging population that is dying off, let alone to bring in church growth. It is time for a fresh start.

Dying for Salt: Two Issues of Social and Moral Decay

The Church has the potential to offer so much to society, particularly in two areas. The first is materialism. It has always existed. It's a natural continuum that with the emergence of more stuff, arises more materialism and greed. How can you blame someone for wanting to provide the best possible life for their family? The face of materialism is often disguised as the pursuit for success and happiness. It is amazing how quickly our desire for "stuff" can take over our lives. We think that if we can acquire more, we will finally be happy. But things do not translate into an easier or happier life. We just feed our appetite for more and more, and perpetuate the vicious cycle. Eventually, nothing will be enough, and it's surprisingly easy to get trapped in an unending quest for more.

Our materialism is making us apathetic to more important things, and causing us to spend money that could be used for more worthy causes such as reducing world hunger. Children, youth and young adults are the generation most impacted. Marketing and ads are directed towards us more aggressively.

Of course, Jesus' message is the total opposite of our obsession with material things. We are called to abandon everything to follow Him. Jesus is the answer to our materialism problem. As Christians in Canada, we could influence our culture to shun much materialism, but first we have to stop being excessively materialistic ourselves.

The second major societal problem that the Church can address is the breakdown of the family. Families don't spend as much time together; divorce is common; relationships are treated as inferior to career; and children are not being disciplined, either appropriately or enough.

As Christ's followers, we can encourage family restoration in our own lives, congregations and communities simply by living our lives as examples and building communities that value relationships above all.

The ministers, priests, and spiritual leaders that my grandfather and his team met with all across Canada had many different thoughts on the question of reversing the moral and social deconstruction of our historical Christian values. These meetings have opened the doors of communication between many pastors and, hopefully, will show fruit by encouraging unity among the many denominations that met together.

This is the very challenging question the participants were asked:

4. In the balance of the prophetic role of the Church and the practical application of truth to daily life, what can the pastors, shepherds, spiritual fathers and mothers do to reverse the moral and social deconstruction of our historical Christian values?

As you read some of the answers, consider if you agree or not, and what your own answer to this question would be.

"We need to strengthen family and home-based fellowships because real transformation begins from families."
~ *Anonymous*

"[There's] no such thing as historical Christian values. There may have been a time when Canadians showed more shame, but Canada has a violent and racist past, i.e. native residential schools."
~ *Rick Chase, Gateway Baptist Church, Surrey, BC*

"Learn to hear and obey the voice of God (understand the word 'prophecy' in its Biblical, as opposed to modern western, meaning). Fast and pray. More children are harmed by heterosexual persons (mostly men) who are willing to pay for sex than by homosexual persons. Address the demand for sex…this demand fuels human trafficking. Address the unending demand for inexpensive consumer products!"
~ *Cornelius Buller, Executive Director of Urban Youth Adventures, Winnipeg, MB*

"It begins with leaders being exemplary – filters through to their families, to their churches. When exemplary lives are lived, quality of life is better. Social ills are decreased. This speaks eloquently. This is our first priority and only until we are an exemplary body can we articulate our position and have broader spiritual impact."

~ David Lee Pong, People's Church, Winnipeg, MB

"Be morally upright and socially responsible. Lead others into the adoption of Christian values. The best endorsement for the Church's values is not logic or political force, but the evidence that these values produce great people of high character. We must reverse the deconstruction in our lives, our homes, our churches, and then we can be salt – actually be different! Salt is primarily a *being* thing – not a *doing* thing. Question is: 'Are we different?' No amount of talking, political advocacy, or anything else will replace being people who actually hold Kingdom values!"

~ Pastor Doug Herbert, Southside Church of the Nazarene, Edmonton, AB

"We need to set our own agenda, not that mandated by the secular media. Over the last few years, the face of the church has been represented by what we are against. We need to effectively communicate what we are for and get this into the mainstream media."

~ Fr. James Mallon, St. Thomas Aquinas Canadian Martyrs, Halifax, NS

"Break down denominational barriers and find ways to partner together in the community."

~ Rev. Gordon Sutherland, Lead Pastor of West End Baptist Church, St. John's, NL

"We need to maintain our commitment to expressing Christ in the larger public square as an expression of our theology without being co-opted by a highly politicized agenda."

~ Dr. Blayne Banting, Briercrest College and Seminary, Caronport, SK

"In some ways, we need to welcome the deconstruction and see it as a rejection of a false gospel that caused people harm. We have a new opportunity to be the Church because every preconception of what the Church has been will not be relevant once people have no first-hand experience of an institutionalized Church."

~ Terry Zimmerly, Grace Mennonite Church, Regina, SK

"We must speak with authority, walk with integrity, and live with an overflowing compassion."

~ Merv Budd, Senior Minister at North Burlington Baptist Church, Burlington, ON

"Do we have historical Christian values, or do we have historical values that were Christian? Were we ever a Christian nation? Is it the goal of the Church to be a Christian nation? Is this founded on the pilgrim history of Kingdom now? What can we do? Be involved in a grassroots movement to influence and encourage Christians to mature and be involved in social justice, politics, good business and community life!"

~ Alan Simpson, Surrey Pastors' Network, Surrey, BC

"...Visible unity among church leaders. We need to spend more time outside our congregational paradigm...make a percentage of pastors' work time to be allotted to community interaction outside the church."

~ Rick Wells, Lead Pastor of The Creek Community Church, Stoney Creek, ON

"Preach Christ, not values and ethics, because Christian values only make sense after conversion/ transformation."

~ Rev. Ray David Glenn, St. George's Anglican Church, Lowville, ON

"Keep praying – keep 'courageo'!" *(This Italian word means "courageous.")*

~ Bishop Fred Henry of Calgary, in a video message shown as a discussion starter.

"We need to meet people where they are so that they are not alienated but open to hearing us. We need to work together in truth. We need to work towards preserving Catholic education. Schools need to be clean – what are they teaching? Lost sense of moral code – we need to use media and influence media. We need to reach out to families and incorporate them into our ministries."

~ *Jenny Tyrcz, St. Dominic Parish, Oakville, ON*

"Reach out to our youth; as we live in a fatherless generation."

~ *Lynn Hazlett, President/CEO of Primex Customs and Logistics, and Founder of The Psalms ministry, Toronto, ON*

"We need to dig down deeper into our faith as church communities so that the Church again overflows with the Spirit. And we have to dig deeper into the roots of our own behaviour so that our lives are also more Christian. The more real we are as Christians, the more credible we will be, and the more we will have to offer the community. The salt needs to rediscover its savour. The Church is not merely an alternative ideology, it is a lived reality which leads to healing and transformation. We need to experience, share and proclaim that. Transformed individuals lead to a transformed society."

~ *Terry Wedge, Christ Church Anglican, Brampton, ON*

"The political process will not recapture the morality that has been lost – you need to change people, one by one. Conversion is not a decision, but means changing our lifestyle. Use deconstruction for our benefit, use the momentum to do good."

~ *Rosemary Redshaw, Chaplain, Church of the Nazarene, Ayr, ON*

"Serve the community in overt, ongoing, and meaningful ways that are perceived to be meaningful to that community, done out of the local churches to their immediate surroundings. In this, people will see the values of the Body of Christ, and see them as personal and valuable – as experienceable. Then they will listen."

~ *Carlo Raponi, Director of Youth Unlimited, Peterborough, ON*

"Maybe it is us who have contributed to the moral and social deconstruction of our historical Christian values. Vatican II occurred because the Church desired to return to the values of the first-century domestic Church. First: where have we gotten off track? We are all part of this problem."

~ Fr. Paul Massel, St. Alphonsus Parish, Peterborough, ON

"The Church should look for opportunities to influence any and all people in positions of leadership. Leadership comes and goes, rises and falls. The Church should avail herself of opportunities to mentor, support, encourage, and influence those who have been chosen to lead, leading by example and encouraging Christians to be involved in all walks of life, including political leadership."

~ Jane Groenewegen, Member of the Legislative Assembly, Hay River South, NWT

"The more real we are as Christians,
the more credible we will be, and the more
we will have to offer the community.
The salt needs to rediscover its savour."

~ Terry Wedge

Chapter 8

Salt in the Kremlin...and Other Surprising Tales

The tour of the Kremlin surprised me. In 1968, my wife Norma-Jean and I were guests in the Soviet Union. The museum housed dozens of the most ornate and precious salt shakers on earth. They were made of gold and silver with exquisite workmanship. Some were studded with diamonds and other precious stones. Custom held that the czar would designate the person he most wished to honour. The guest would have no idea until he was ushered to his place at the table whether his dinner plate was placed just behind the salt.

In Roman society, salt was used as currency. Soldiers were paid in it, hence the saying, "He is worth his salt." The Latin word "sal" is the root for the English word "salary." Salt was so very precious and rare, it was often brought by caravan from the Himalayan mountains. When Jesus announced in Matthew 5:13, *"You are the salt of the earth,"* people realized how much Jesus valued His followers.

Back at the Kremlin, we were introduced to five churches inside the Kremlin walls. Stalin, the one-time seminarian, an atheist who murdered millions, lived there behind those walls. I had no idea that the centre of world atheism would have churches. After all, Lenin said, "Even the thought of God is utter vileness."

I learned that while Lenin was making his sea-change speech in Red Square, the clergy were engaged in a loud argument about the width of the embroidery on their robes. One of the Kremlin churches had a hole in the wall. The guide pointed out that Czar Ivan, who made Henry VIII look good, had been excommunicated from the cathedral where he was the only person (other than the priest) allowed on the main floor. His czarina (wife) and their children sat in the balcony. Ivan was so "religious" that he had the hole cut in the wall and, even at minus 20° C, he would stand outside to observe the liturgy for all its two hours.

The first night in Moscow at the Metropole Hotel, I couldn't sleep. It was still evening at home. According to *Reader's Digest,* this hotel had more peepholes and more microphones than *Radio Moscow.* This was where Corrie Ten Boom's *Salt and Pepper* messages were written. She purposely spoke them into the pinholes of the wall, suspecting that there were microphones behind them. About 2 a.m. I arose, dressed and walked over to Red Square where the guard goose-stepped back and forth before Lenin's tomb. At the other end of the square was the multi onion-domed St. Bazil's Cathedral. St. Bazil's was built by Czar Ivan the Terrible to celebrate his victory over the Muslim Tartars. Which represented the greater tragedy, the magnificent cathedral or Lenin's mausoleum?

I visited the Soviet Union several times in the intervening years. Then, in 1990, I was honoured to preach for two nights to at least 1,200 Christian leaders from all 15 republics of the Soviet Union. For the first time, the government allowed such a gathering. Yes, there were Baptists, Pentecostals and, to my delight, Orthodox priests. My final message was, "The Church after persecution ceases." That night, I received hundreds of kisses, as is their custom, right on the lips (God gave me grace). Some of those kisses came from bushy-bearded priests and monks, many of whom were preaching the Gospel on the streets.

One day, as I was preparing my message, a knock came to the door. I opened it and saw a big man, whom I recognized as security for the hotel, holding a large box. Out from behind came a small man who reached into the box, took out a book, entered the room and put it in the drawer of my bedside table. It was a Gideon Bible. At that moment, I knew that salty Christians were infiltrating the U.S.S.R. and atheism was losing its grip.

What I saw during my visit was that salt was permeating Soviet society, and the light was shining brightly. One of my most meaningful experiences came while the Soviet Socialist Republic of Armenia was still intact. A horrific earthquake had killed thousands. Crossroads raised the money to purchase new medical equipment for the children's hospital in Yerevan. We took Dr. Rosa to Sweden where she walked the aisles of a huge warehouse, choosing equipment.

A few months later, Dr. Rosa took me through the newly equipped hospital. Surgeons were repairing an area of the brain of a 13-year-old boy whose head had been partially crushed by a falling piece of concrete. The equipment, a high magnification monitor, made it possible.

Then the doctor introduced me to a 12-year-old girl. Six months earlier, her mother and father had been crushed to death by a collapsing wall, and her young brother also died a horrific death. The girl was not physically damaged, but was so traumatized that she hadn't uttered a word since. Now she was in the psychiatric ward. The doctor spoke from the door and told me that the girl had studied English for five years. Turning to the girl, she said, "This is the man who provided your bed." I quickly pointed out that, in fact, it was many people from Canada who had done this.

I then took the girl's hand and asked, "Do you believe in God?" She shook her head "no." So I responded, "I believe in God. Would you like me to ask God to make you well?" She nodded "yes." I slipped to my knees, still holding her hand and prayed, "Dear God, please make this precious child well." I had forgotten to ask Dr. Rosa the girl's name. What happened at this point was perhaps the most moving moment of my life. She held my hand more tightly, sat up in bed and spoke these words, "My name is Laura." Wham! An emotional tide hit me. I bent over, kissed her and departed to continue the tour. All the Canadians providing the money to buy the beds and equipment were truly salty.

"Then one day, I can't explain it any other way, I met Jesus of Nazareth in a powerful visitation. On the spot, I was converted to be His forever."

~ Armenian Orthodox Patriarch of Yerevan

In the same visit to Armenia, I was told by a Pentecostal pastor that just a few weeks earlier, the KGB had arrived at his church, just as he was closing his Sunday evening service. He was arrested and taken to prison. To his surprise, the Baptist pastor was already there in the cell. A few minutes later, the cell door opened and the same guard ushered the Armenian

Orthodox Patriarch of Yerevan. They sat there without a word for an awkward five minutes or so.

Then the patriarch spoke. "I confess that I arranged your arrests. It was the only way I could get your attention. While still in my 20s, I was the leader of the Young Communists of Armenia. I took pleasure in persecuting all the leaders of all the churches. Then one day, I can't explain it any other way, I met Jesus of Nazareth in a powerful visitation. On the spot, I was converted to be His forever. I attended the only seminary there was, Orthodox. Now I'm the patriarch. I am your brother. You've got to stop attacking me. I desire just as much as you do to reach my Armenian people with the Good News of Jesus. We must begin to work together!" For once, the pastors were speechless until they embraced each other and wept.

The sequel is that the patriarch sent his two most brilliant priests to our Crossroads Conway School of Broadcasting in Burlington, Ontario, where they graduated with the highest marks in the 26-year history of the school. I've not seen it personally, but I understand that the patriarch has a TV station now with a transmitter on Mt. Ararat. He's broadcasting, not only to his own people, but also to the Turks on the other side of the mountain.

Chapter 9

Salt at Home

Approximately 15 years ago, I did a series of daily four-minute segments on the *100 Huntley Street* telecast. I spent an entire year on the longest recorded homily Jesus gave, the Sermon on the Mount. The message explains what Jesus meant by "salt." From these teachings, Crossroads published a book titled, *Going the Extra Smile.* Peter Stec, a professional photographer, took photos to illustrate the various segments. Do you remember the *Maggie and Jiggs* comic strip? They were my inspiration for the large, poster-sized photos we included with each teaching.

My elder son, David Reynold Mainse, researched diligently to help me with this TV series. Reynold is now leading the missions charge for Crossroads/*100 Huntley Street* and is also president of a broad-based, multi-denominational ministry known as *World Embrace.* Reynold and his wife Kathy, who host *100 Huntley Street* on Mondays, led a most unique event known as *Heaven's Rehearsal,* which was held in Toronto on September 15, 2007. Reynold and Kathy sat in the upper stands and were not recognized in any way, either from the platform, in print, or in the amazing DVD and CD produced from the three-hour event. In fact, no participants were named. The only name mentioned was the name that is above every name (Philippians 2:9); the only name given under heaven among men whereby we must be saved (Acts 4:12).

In the summer of 2003, my younger son, Ron, was named president of the Crossroads Family of Ministries. This not only includes the daily one-hour *100 Huntley Street* program but also the nine youth camps that comprise Circle Square Ranch. There are other television productions such as the *NiteLite* live, open-line telecast which airs seven nights a week on CTS. There are also children's telecasts and the ministry of Crossroads' 24-hour toll-free prayer line that receives more than 1,000 telephone calls every day. World Missions is another top priority for Crossroads Christian

Communications Incorporated.

One would be forgiven for expecting some sibling rivalry when the younger brother is selected to be president, and both brothers and their wives work in the ministry. Here is something amazing to me. I entered the Green Room (the preparation room before going on air) several weeks before the board of directors of Crossroads appointed the younger son Ron as president. (I should mention that I refused to attend any of the board meetings when the succession was being discussed). I was amazed to find Kathy, Reynold's wife, on her knees in front of Ron. She was weeping. I heard her say, "Ron, God has called Reynold and me to serve you." Would you agree that God honours that kind of humility?

Kathy and Ann, Reynold's and Ron's wives, were roommates in university. They would lie awake and talk of their dreams of being married to the Mainse boys and living around the corner from each other. That's exactly what happened! Reynold and Ron are close to each other as well. One day, while they were in Grades 12 and 13 at Gordon Graydon Secondary School in Mississauga, their principal, David Craig, called me asking if I could drop by his office. Mr. Craig proceeded to tell me that he had taken their files from the guidance counsellor in order to help direct the boys. He said that no matter what he suggested for career options, he could only get out of the boys, "We want to work with our father."

I knew nothing of this before. That afternoon I waited in the living room for them to arrive home. "Come here," I said, telling them what their principal had informed me of earlier. Reynold and Ron looked apprehensive. I proceeded to explain: "I have never even hinted at the possibility of you both working with me – not because I wouldn't want you, but because I didn't want you to feel obligated in any way. If God calls you, you will know it. So will I, and so will others. You need to know that I will never hire you, give you a raise or a promotion. Others – staff or board members – will have to do this or people will accuse you of getting a position because of your father and not because of God's call or your merits."

I wept. We hugged. And I'm dumbfounded by what God has done. Norma-Jean, who was senior producer for *100 Huntley Street* at the time, came home, expressed joy after hearing the story, made supper for the family, and life went on. Our two daughters, Elaine Stacey and Ellen Shaheen, are wonderful supporters too. They often tell me: "Dad, you've got to put your stories in a book. There are dozens of events that could never have happened unless God was involved."

The odds against these things happening apart from God are astronomical. Often, we can see His work in our lives – His salt happening, if you will – within our own families. Take a moment and think about how you have seen salt at work amongst those closest to you.

Sarah, my co-author, would not be here if it were not for what our family regards as a supernatural happening. I call her my "Brussels' Sprout." It was May of 1985. Her father, Nizar Shaheen, an Arab-Israeli Christian who is now ordained in the Nazareth Baptist Church, was a theological student in Brussels at the time. Our daughter Ellen, Sarah's mother, was hanging clothes out on the balcony of their high-rise apartment. She had placed some toys out on the balcony for one-year-old Sarah's playtime. It was a beautiful late spring day. The railing around the balcony was made of strong Plexiglass™, with an opening of mere inches at the bottom.

A pot of potatoes on the stove had boiled over and Ellen quickly rushed inside to tend to them. The diversion took just a few seconds. However, when Ellen returned, all she saw of Sarah were her fingertips clutching onto the edge of the high balcony. Her little one had slipped under the Plexiglass™ and was hanging on for her life. Sarah's eyes peeked over the edge, level with the floor. Thinking about it, even now, makes Ellen cry.

Slowly, Ellen moved toward Sarah, careful not to frighten her. "Let Mommy hold you," she said. She then took Sarah's little hands and pulled her small body back through the opening. Ellen believes, as we do, that an angel was already holding her. Ellen hugged her baby girl and cried for the longest time.

It is my hope that this book, and the insights from Christian leaders across Canada, has helped you in your own commitment to being salt – in your family, in your work, in your church, in your ministry and, most of all, in the world where Jesus calls us to be. To help you grow even deeper in this subject, you are invited to embark on a 30-day study period and meditate on the following devotionals. They are inspired from Jesus' description of what salt looks like.

Appendix A

In preparation for the Salt 2007 tour, I contacted both church and political leaders for words of encouragement for the process. I'd like to share a couple of them with you. First, let's hear from Stephen Harper, Prime Minister of Canada. This message was played at every gathering during the Salt 2007 tour.

Prime Minister Stephen Harper's Message

"Thanks, David, for the invitation to briefly join your meeting. As Canadians, we are fortunate to live in a society in which we have the right to choose our leaders. In fact, one of the oldest and most enduring values we have in this country is democracy, a principle that allows us to change our government without risking our freedoms or our lives.

"It is this freedom that brought many of our ancestors from different nationalities, backgrounds and faiths to this country. It is a freedom we must always cherish as Canadians, and the best way to protect this hard-won freedom is to exercise it. The power should belong to all of the people – not just some – and this includes the members of Canada's faith communities.

"Companies, unions and special interest groups have the ability and the resources to hire people and to push their agendas. The only tool available to most people is the power of their ballot. Canada is a multi-cultural and pluralist society, but this doesn't mean that faith should be excluded from the public square. On the contrary. People of different faiths should be able to work together for the common good.

"So no matter who you are, where you're from, what your beliefs, or which party you support, the important thing for you to do is to get informed, participate, and get out and vote. Make your voices heard and ensure that your values and principles are represented by your leaders. I want to thank you for your time. God bless you in all of your efforts, and God bless Canada."

I regard Bishop Frederick Henry of the Roman Catholic Diocese of Calgary a most salty person. In preparation for the Salt 2007 tour across Canada, I asked the bishop to videotape a message to ministers, priests and other Christian leaders. Here's that message.

Bishop Frederick Henry's Message

"I think our duty and responsibility is to unmask some of the false conceptions about humanity that are present in our society and, in addition to that, we have to defend some of the values that seem to be under attack. We have to discern the truth, preach the Gospel and, above all, be people who are prepared to stand up and be somewhat prophetic.

"Our Saviour has called us to be salt and light to the world. You will recall that, in July of 2005, the previous government radically changed the definition of marriage, and we moved from recognition of a voluntary union between a man and a woman for life to a voluntary union between two persons, including two men or two women. Many people in our society today are saying, 'Well, the sky didn't fall.' Much of the modern media is saying, 'Let's not re-open this issue of question.' And some people even downtown are saying: 'It hasn't affected me; my life hasn't changed in any way. Everything is as normal as it used to be.' On the other hand, I want to raise a few points that indicate there have been some adverse effects as the result of what has transpired last July.

"I would point, first of all, to the change in the society, in terms of our understanding of the homosexual lifestyle. Now it is being presented as something that is wholesome – something that is normal – whereas we all know the facts indicate that it is unwholesome and it is immoral.

"At the recent international conference on AIDS in Toronto, we heard an awful lot of talk on pills and prophylactics, but very few people talked about the nature of sexuality and the need for a conversion of lifestyle. Since July of last year, we have also found that those who dare to speak up opposing same-sex marriage are having some of their freedoms challenged, and some of us have had the experience of being hauled before human rights tribunals and human right legislation which was designed at one time to be a shield. It is now being used as a sword.

"In addition to that, we find out that children now can legally be adopted by gay and lesbian parents, and little thought is given to the child and what is in their best interest. We have seen, in addition to that, a change in much of the curriculum affecting some of our schools. Recently, in British Columbia, a homosexual couple has been given almost the entire responsibility of censorship in the design of the curriculum that is to deal with social studies and, of course, their own particular agenda is going to be uppermost in their mind. I could go on and talk about a number of different items that are impinging upon our freedoms and indicating that our society is radically changing. Nevertheless, there are some real signs of hope.

"Whenever a poll is conducted of the average citizens in our country of Canada, we find that the majority – the overwhelming majority – are opposed to same-sex marriage. At the same time, we find that they are consistent in their reasons why – because there is no gender complementarity, there is no openness to the procreation of children, and it is fundamentally opposed to the natural law.

"There is a small voice, and yet a powerful one, that is advocating another agenda. That other agenda I think can be seen reflected in a private member's bill that was at least taken seriously by some in the House of Commons last year, in which they sought to expand once again Section 15 of the Canadian Human Rights Charter to include transgendered and transvestite people, affording them recognition and equality in all aspects of the law.

"We've also seen the Supreme Court of Canada change the legislation with respect to community standards. In Labaye versus the Attorney General, all of a sudden it was decided that swingers' clubs (which involve the swapping of partners and public orgies) are now legal. It isn't too far of a stretch to see that, in the near future, someone will come forward advocating a change in the status of polygamy and polyandry.

"As believers and as Christians, we stand in the face of a tremendous onslaught to our morality. A lot of false thinking is out there that goes unchallenged. It strikes me that it is a part of our responsibility to no longer remain silent but, first of all – in terms of our pulpits – to speak up and enunciate the truth (the truth of the Gospel) and to celebrate the sanctity of marriage and family life.

"In addition to our own responsibilities as leaders and preachers of the Good News, we also have to be prepared to mobilize our lay people to push back. The majority are opposed to same-sex marriage and yet, for some reason, they seem to be inclined to want to sit on their hands and not become politically involved. I don't think Jesus left us that option. He called us to be "salt and light" for the world. We are never going to convert the world – we are never going to evangelize properly – unless we begin to witness to authentic values.

"Finally, I think it is our responsibility also to encourage our lay people, both men and women, to run for public office. There is no higher vocation outside of the ministry itself than that of the politician. We need statesmen and stateswomen today who will stand up with integrity and with conviction, who will recognize their responsibilities as true humanists, who are men and women of culture and the arts, who are scientifically alert and aware of the most modern developments, and yet who are prepared to serve not only their country but to serve God Himself.

"I could think of no finer example to hold up than the witness of St. Thomas Moore, someone who was fully conversive with the needs of the society and who was committed to serving the king. He was the king's loyal servant, but God's first. I think that is part of our challenge to find that kind of person to run for public office. No matter what happens this coming fall on the question of same-sex marriage, and how the vote will go, if we begin to think long range (which I think we must begin to do), we have to build marriage and family life. Yet we also have to cultivate those kinds of people who can best serve the country of Canada and, at the same time, give honour and glory to God.

"Jesus said in the Gospel of John that there will be fear in the world but that He wanted us to be people of good joy because He has overcome the world. In a word, I would urge all of you, as one of my Italian friends would say, 'Courageo' ('courageous'), we win in the end. Courageo!"

Becoming Salt

A 30-Day Journey Into Scripture

The backlit salt crystal featured on the front cover of this book is from the Himalayan mountains. It was presented to David Mainse in 2006 on his 70th birthday and represents the call of believers to be "salt and light."

Day 1

Skinned Knees
Matthew 5:4

Often on distant journeys that go on for more than a few days, we encounter difficulties or what we refer to as "bad times." And so it is with our journey in becoming the salt of the earth. As we live out our days, we are bound to experience sorrow, pain, and times of mourning. Perhaps you are saying, "That's me!" Let me assure you that constant joy can be yours despite circumstances. We must not think that joy only comes when we smile. Joy can also come through our tears.

When we are hurt, there comes a point when we make it known. We want comfort. Comfort soothes, heals, and says – with or without words – "It's going to be all right."

When my children were young they would need comfort after skinning a knee. Those were close and wonderful times. What a wonderful feeling *to* comfort, and what a wonderful feeling *to be* comforted. And now with 16 grandchildren I'm often saying, "Grandpa can kiss it and make it all better."

There is a wise saying by those who live in hot and sand-swept regions: "All sunshine makes a desert." Think about it. The land on which the sun always shines will soon become an arid place in which no fruit will grow. There are certain things which only the rains can produce.

Here's a thought-provoking poem:

> "I walked a mile with Pleasure,
> She chattered all the way,
> But left me none the wiser,
> For all she had to say.

> "I walked a mile with Sorrow,
> And ne'er a word said she,
> But, oh, the things I learned from her
> When Sorrow walked with me!"

It is the shallow life that has only smiled. The person who has the greatest understanding and the ability to touch people with compassion is the person who has been touched by both extremes of happiness and sorrow. That is the person who knows what it is really like to be salt in a world desperate for it. Jesus experienced both, and He can comfort like no other. Matthew 5:4 says, *"Blessed are those who mourn, for they shall be comforted."*

You may be mourning. You may be filled with sorrow. Your heart may be heavy. Receive comfort. Receive it from a friend, a family member, or even from these words of comfort. Jesus said, *"Come to Me, all you who labour and are heavy laden, and I will give you rest"* (Matthew 11:28). He promises a constant flowing joy that will never run dry. It will well up from inside you, whatever the inner pain or outer circumstance.

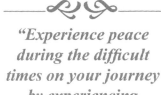

"Experience peace during the difficult times on your journey by experiencing God's comfort along the way."

You may feel it's going to take a lot of tempering to become "salty"...and that may be. But be assured that many have walked the same road as you and have arrived a better person. So can you!

Experience peace during the difficult times on your journey by experiencing God's comfort along the way.

Meekness Not Weakness
Matthew 5:5

Today's step in our journey into becoming the salt of the earth is *"strength under control."*

J. Upton Dickson was a fun-loving fellow who talked of writing a book titled, *Cower Power.* He also founded a group for submissive people. It was called DOORMATS. The acrostic stands for: Dependent, Organization Of Really Meek And Timid Souls. Their motto was: "The meek shall inherit the earth – if that's okay with everybody." Their symbol was the yellow traffic light.

Mr. Dickson sounds like he would be a lot of fun. However, what is disturbing about all of this is that many people assume the ridiculous ideas behind DOORMATS and *Cower Power* represent the quality of meekness. Christians know that meekness is an essential ingredient in joyful living.

In our modern use of English, the word "meek" is often mistaken to mean "spineless." It paints the picture of a submissive and ineffective creature. But the word "meek," when originally used in the English language, meant much more. Meek in the Bible is translated from the Greek word "praus," which was one of the great Greek ethical words.

"We could say then that the word 'meek,' this essential ingredient for being salt and light, is described as: A person who is well-balanced in nature and always angry at the right time and never angry at the wrong time...."

The Greek philosopher Aristotle had a practice of defining every virtue as a mid-point between two extremes. He defined meekness as the mid-point between excessive anger and excessive apathy in the face of injustice. He saw it as being well-balanced; a happy medium between too much and too little anger.

Aristotle made this wise observation: "Anybody can become angry – that is easy. But to be angry with the right person, to the right degree, at the right time, for the right purpose, and in the right way – that is not easy!"

A second Greek usage for the word "praus" was attributed to an animal that had been domesticated and trained to obey and, as a result, showed great self-control. It was the lack of this quality of self-control which ruined Alexander the Great who, in a fit of uncontrolled temper while drunk, hurled a spear at his best friend and killed him. Also, in a fit of anger, Stalin died from coronary occlusion.

We could say then that the word "meek," this essential ingredient for being salt and light, is described as: "A person who is well-balanced in nature and always angry at the right time and never angry at the wrong time; one who has every instinct, impulse and passion under control."

In Matthew 5:5, Jesus says, *"Blessed are the meek, for they shall inherit the earth."* Meekness is not weakness but *strength under control* – strength that is harnessed by wisdom. It's an essential element of being the salt that Jesus has asked us to be in a hurting world. Cultivating meekness in your life will bring you more respect, appreciation, favour and, of course, you will be "saltier" for it!

"Anybody can become angry – that is easy. But to be angry with the right person, to the right degree, at the right time, for the right purpose, and in the right way – that is not easy!"
~ *Aristotle*

Day 3

Who Gave the Ability to Laugh
Matthew 5:12

"Rejoice and be exceedingly glad, for great is your reward in heaven..." (Matthew 5:12).

The typical child laughs 150 times daily. The average adult chuckles only 15 times a day. Scientific research links laughter to reductions of immune suppressors such as epinephrine and cortisol. Laughter positively affects hormone and white cell counts, and increases activity of disease-fighting cells. Laughter increases heart rate, raises blood pressure, speeds breathing and increases oxygen consumption. After laughing, your heart rate slows, your blood pressure lowers and muscles relax. Laughter also has been shown to raise pain tolerance, even with obstetrical patients. In general, a positive and cheerful approach to life's inconsistencies increases healing and resistance.

Laughter is a wonderful gift from God. In Psalm 126 it is connected with songs of praise to the Lord. Through it, the Israelites expressed their joy for the opportunity to return home after decades of captivity.

During the Civil War, Abraham Lincoln was criticized for his humour. He replied, "With the fearful strain that is on me, if I did not laugh, I should die!" Laughter is good for releasing tension and can meet a real need in our lives. Proverbs 17:22 tells us, *"A merry heart does good, like medicine."*

What does laughter have to do with being salt? Healthy churches love to laugh together. Just as music brings a church together in the unity of harmony, laughter creates a unity of joy. Churches need a corporate sense of humour. I am convinced that a church's morale can be measured by the amount of joy present when we come together and laugh. An old war-horse preacher one said, "When things get really tough, certainly call a prayer meeting, but also get everyone together to laugh about the tough stuff."

A positive step in our journey into influencing society is to put all our present difficulties and persecutions in the light of God's future eternal blessing. By doing this you will be lifted and will rejoice with joyous laughter, leaving the despair behind. Your joy will break down walls so that you can positively influence your world!

Day 4

Spice of Life
Matthew 5:13

Salt is the stuff of history. It is so vital to human survival that wars have been fought over it, empires have been founded on it and have collapsed without it, and civilizations have grown up around it. Humankind realized from the earliest days that, without salt, we would perish. Without it in our bodies, the delicate salt and water balance is upset, and dehydration hastens death.

Even the word "salary" is a constant reminder of its importance. Roman legionaries were given a "salarium" – a salt allowance. Later, the word came to mean a cash allowance to buy salt. The word "salary" stemmed from this word.

As a boy, I remember my parents cutting meat in small pieces and placing it in boiling hot jars with liberal portions of salt. The jars were made airtight by the cooling process. The Mainse family had meat all year without the need of refrigeration.

The function of God's people living in a world that disowns God is to prevent it from going completely bad. We are given the responsibility of preserving all that is good, kind, loving, pure and true in our world and society.

During our first trip to the Kremlin in Russia, my wife Norma-Jean and I were amazed to see what were obviously the most fabulous salt shakers ever crafted. They were of ingenious design and many were encrusted with jewels. We learned that when the czars, the aristocracy and other wealthy citizens of Imperial Russia were giving a formal dinner, they would place the salt shaker in front of the person judged most worthy of honour. That is why sitting "next to the salt" was a very desirable place to be!

Jesus was accused of eating and drinking with publicans and sinners. I can imagine that there was a rush to sit next to Him. Jesus says about us who represent Him, *"You are the salt of the earth"* (Matthew 5:13). As we take our journey, one step at a time, we can be transformed into salty and attractive people. Those searching for the truth will want to sit "next to the salt."

Day 5

Hit the Switch

Matthew 5:14a

The world will be a brighter or a darker place because of our influence on it. We need to "hit the switch" and let our lights shine brightly. This is a tall order. How can we possibly be light in such a dark world? Most of us feel that our influence is little and our light does not make a dramatic difference. How wrong we are. Light is always more powerful than darkness. In fact, there isn't enough darkness in the entire world to put out the light of a single candle.

When we think of light, we immediately imagine an electric light bulb filling the whole room with brightness. This is not the way it is in our daily lives. Notice a sunrise. Before the sun appears, its influence is felt. Slowly, almost mystically, a subtle change begins to take place in the world. The darkness loosens its grip on the earth and begins to dissolve into day. As the sun rises higher in the sky, all the darkness is gone and the world of fear and the unknown is soon filled with beautiful trees, running brooks, and towering mountains. What a difference the light makes. The despair of the night is overwhelmed by the dawning of light.

Let us, together, decide to shine. The way to shine is *to love*. How do we learn to live and love? Emmet Fox wisely said these words: "There is no difficulty that enough love will not conquer; no disease that enough love will not heal; no door that enough love will not open; no gulf that enough love will not bridge; no sin that enough love will not redeem. It makes no difference how deeply-seated the trouble may be or how hopeless the outlook, how muddled the tangle, how great the mistake. Because a sufficient realization of love will dissolve it all. If only you could love enough, you would be one of the happiest and most powerful beings in the world."

Darkness cannot drive out darkness. Only light can. Hate cannot drive out hate. Only love can. Let's return to the source of all love – *Jesus*. He reminds of this important fact: *"You are the light of the world"* (Matthew 5:14a). In other words, you are the salt. And, at times, when your salt shaker feels empty in the struggle to get by in day-to-day life, be assured that He has an unlimited supply awaiting you. His salt always flavours!

Day 6

In Plain View
Matthew 5:14b

Could you ever imagine a powerful international leader directing his attention to you and speaking these words, "You, yes, YOU are the light of the world." You might shake your head in disbelief and ask, "Are you sure you have got the right person?" He responds, "Yes, you are like a city on a hill that cannot be hidden." Perhaps in disbelief you would ponder, "How can this be?"

If you love good, you represent good. Just as a lighthouse shines in the darkness giving light, guidance, and warning, this world is in great need of people who will prove what is good and acceptable. The *"King of kings"* and *"Lord of lords"* did announce: *"You are the light of the world. A city that is set on a hill cannot be hidden."* Jesus says this about each one of His followers who come to realize where the source of good comes from. We are to be reflectors of His light and goodness. We are to be salt.

There was a woman who felt very much alone at her place of employment because she was the only professing Christian. To make matters worse, she was often ridiculed for her faith and accused of being narrow-minded. Finally, she became so discouraged that she considered quitting her job. Before doing that, however, she sought the counsel of her pastor. After listening to her complaints, the minister asked, "Where do people usually put lights?" She replied, "In dark places." No sooner had the words escaped her lips when she realized how her answer applied to her own life. She quickly recognized that her place of work was indeed a "dark place" where "light" was vitally needed, so she decided to stay where she was and become a stronger influence for Christ. She determined to be salt in her workplace.

Often, we may not realize that, with each drop of kindness or cruelty, there are waves of ever-widening circles that touch many lives. We are either bringing light to the world or allowing darkness to continue.

A step in our journey into being effective salt and light is to realize and accept the fact that God wants you to represent Him. In so doing, He will impart radiance to your human heart. Remember, He needs you and this world needs you!

Day 7

This Little Light of Mine
Matthew 5:15

Children are entertaining, aren't they? And they are also very impressionable. I think of the father who was scowling over his son's very bad report card. The son piped up and asked: "What do you think it is, Dad? Heredity or environment?"

An enjoyable part of becoming salt and light is to invest in family relationships. It's never too late to start. Let's not be so busy preparing *the path for our children*. Rather, let's be busy preparing *our children for the path*. Spend time and energy in shaping that little life. Take advantage of those impressionable years. I heard a poem titled, *Living Clay,* which tells of the impact we can have on a life.

"I took a piece of plastic clay
And idly fashioned it one day;
And as my fingers pressed it still,
It moved and yielded to my will.
I came again when days were past,
The bit of clay was hard at last;
The form I gave it, it still bore,
But I could change that form no more.

"I took a piece of living clay
And gently formed it day by day,
And molded with my power and art
A young child's soft and yielding heart.
I came again when years were gone
It was a man I looked upon;
He still that early impress wore,
And I could change him nevermore."

You will never regret the time you spend with your child. However, you will regret the time you don't. Don't fret about the past. Make the most of the present, for that is where your child lives. Jesus taught in Matthew 5:15: *"No one lights a lamp and then puts it under a basket. Instead, a lamp is placed on a stand, where it gives light for everyone in the house"* (NLT).

As believers, we are called *"the light of the world."* Being a light in the world first begins at home. Take the time and show an interest. One of the most important truths I can tell you is that the role of "Mummy" or "Daddy" represents God in the hearts of children. Therefore, let's seriously consider our relationship with each of our children, especially during those formative years, realizing that this relationship will greatly affect their adult relationship with God. So represent God well, and model the ways you want your child to be. Be salt to your child, and your child will be salt to the world.

"One of the most important truths I can tell you is that the role of 'Mummy' or 'Daddy' represents God in the hearts of children."

Day 8

Walk of Faith
Matthew 5:16

Our next practical step towards being the salt of the earth is to be part of the solution and not the problem. We can have a positive impact on the world around us if we open our eyes to a need and meet it.

At Crossroads, this has been our great focus: To meet needs and serve all people. Jesus did not say, "You are the light of the church." Rather He said, *"You are the light of the world"* (5:14). We are called to be salt in the world, not just inside our congregations. We take that very seriously. Everything we and our partners do is geared towards bringing people to a closer understanding of who Jesus is, and how He can make a meaningful difference in their lives.

One of the greatest proofs that this ministry lets its light shine before men is a document we received several years ago from the province of Ontario, for which I am very thankful. It concerned the property tax that we had been paying for our downtown Toronto location. As a result of a legislative bill, the money we had paid was returned to Crossroads and we were exempted from any further property tax, providing the owners of the building would pass the savings on to Crossroads.

"Jesus did not say, 'You are the light of the church.' Rather He said, 'You are the light of the world'"

~ Matthew 5:14

The government justice committee had an opportunity for a hearing prior to making this decision. Some members had examples in their ridings of people who had been helped: reconciled family members, young people delivered from drugs, runaways who returned home, and alcoholics who sobered up.

Crossroads/*100 Huntley Street* had provided such a social service to the people, it was resolved that the province would exempt us from paying realty tax. It was totally without precedent. In the history of

96

Ontario, it had never happened before. To my knowledge, it has not happened since.

The government of Ontario recognized that there were good works being accomplished through *100 Huntley Street* due to the television ministry, the telephone prayer lines and the follow-up of the local churches. It is because of faithful partners who support this ministry through prayer and giving, we are able to fulfill this commandment: *"Let your light so shine before men, that they may see your good works and glorify your Father in heaven"* (Matthew 5:16).

Jesus admonishes us to shine and do good works. He needs you, He needs me, and He needs us to work together. Let's put God's kingdom before ours and continue being the salt that Jesus said we are to be...becoming part of the solutions to the problems of human need.

"Let your light so shine before men, that they may see your good works and glorify your Father in heaven."
~ Matthew 5:16

Day 9

Truth or Consequences
Matthew 5:18

There used to be a fun game show on television called, *Truth or Consequences*. It may be off the air now, but we are still playing it! I remember an episode in my life as a nine-year-old in the village of Madoc, Ontario, when I went into business for the first time. I cut Christmas trees from a field just outside the village and hauled them one at a time on my toboggan from door to door, selling them at a bargain to delighted buyers. With great joy, I bounced home to tell my parents about my success. With the money in my hand, my happiness slowly drained away as the look on Dad's face indicated I'd done something wrong. He asked me where I got the trees. I answered, "Well, in a field." He further questioned, "What field?" I continued hesitantly, "In a farmer's field." Dad then told me the gripping reality that I had actually stolen the trees.

Dad put me in the car. We were going to make the wrong, right. I could have crawled under the seat, I felt so small. At my Dad's prompting, I asked for the forgiveness of the farmer. I was hoping the farmer would pat me on the head and say, "That's all right, little fellow. Keep the money." But he didn't, and I was broke once again.

My father knew the truth. I, too, learned the truth that day, and it was underscored by the consequences. After the embarrassment and remorse over the loss of the money wore off, I felt enlightened. I actually felt better. Jesus said, *"You shall know the truth, and the truth shall set you free"* (John 8:32).

To be effective as salt, we must face the truth and make our wrongs, right. Then we would be wise to learn from our mistakes and live according to the truth, thus avoiding future consequences.

Finally, the One who taught, *"I am the way, the truth and the life"* (John 14:6), also explained that the Law (truth) shall not lose one single dot or comma until its purpose is complete (Matthew 5:18).

A journey of 1,000 miles starts with one step. You can do it. This journey is worthwhile. Your presence as salt is essential.

Day 10

Walk Your Talk
Matthew 5:19

One of the greatest things you can say about a person is, "What you see, is what you get." In this statement, honesty and sincerity are implied. The opposite of these is hypocrisy. That beautiful-on-the-outside and rotten-on-the-inside type of life is not something any of us desire. The phrase, "Do as I say, but don't do as I do," just doesn't work! Especially when you are trying to be salt.

A young Christian businessman from Nashville was invited to speak at a local church. He chose for his text, *"Thou shalt not steal,"* and he spoke unswervingly on the topic. The next morning he boarded a city bus for his ride to work. He handed a dollar bill to the driver and received some change, which he counted as he proceeded down the aisle of the bus. Before reaching his seat, he realized he had been given a dime too much.

His first thought was that the transit company would never miss it. But deep inside he knew he should return it. So he went back to the driver and said, "You gave me too much change." To the businessman's amazement, the driver replied with these words: "I know. A dime too much. I gave it to you on purpose. Then I watched you in my mirror as you counted your change. You see, I heard you speak yesterday. If you had kept the dime, I would have had no confidence in what you said."

Jesus said, *"...whoever practises and teaches [these commandments] will be called great in the kingdom of heaven"* (Matthew 5:19 HCSB). This is a world of compromise and broken agreements, where black and white are covered in gray. Though this is all around us, we can experience great joy in living the truth, walking our talk, and having nothing to hide.

As pure and effective salt, we must make sure our actions line up with our beliefs and words. Doing this reaps the reward of respect from family members, friends, yourself, and even your foe. Let's be people of integrity – seasoning this world with truth and honesty.

Agree to Agree
Matthew 5:25a

As children, we mumble it. As adults, we fumble it. What is it? The words, "I'm sorry." This is a powerful statement that can calm a tumultuous quarrel. It can prove that you are salt.

An honoured tradition every Christmas for our family is watching the movie, *A Christmas Carol* (better known as *Scrooge)*, by Charles Dickens. After Scrooge was with the ghost of Christmas past, present, and future, he realizes that his greed and bitterness have made himself and others miserable. Most of all, he realizes the importance of loving relationships.

As Scrooge wakes clinging to his bedpost curtains, he determines to change and positively effect the future, especially that of Tiny Tim. I think one of the classic lines that we would do well to learn from is when Scrooge unexpectedly drops in on his nephew's well-attended Christmas Day party. He then says to his nephew and his nephew's wife, to the delight and astonishment of all, "Can you forgive the pig-headed old fool for having no eyes to see with and no ears to hear with all these years?" These sincere, humble words reconciled Scrooge to his family. Words spoken with the right attitude can initiate healing in fractured relationships and put to rest simple disputes.

"Then we need to own up to our mistakes – the ways in which we have hurt others. At this point, we can complete this step in being true salt by reconciling strained relationships."

At the conclusion of the movie, we see Scrooge sitting alone in his office after overwhelming Bob Cratchit with kindness and generosity. Being overwhelmed himself by the changes in his life, Scrooge says out loud, "Oh, I don't deserve to be so happy, but I just can't help it!"

We also can experience being an object of grace as depicted by Scrooge if we are willing, at the prompting and guidance of the Holy Spirit, to take a good look at ourselves in the light of God's presence and word. Then we need to own up to our mistakes – the ways in which we have hurt others. At this point, we can complete this step in being true salt by reconciling strained relationships.

There was a stubborn old farmer who was plowing his field. A neighbour was watching as the farmer tried to guide the mule. Finally the neighbour interjected, "I don't want to butt in, but you could save yourself a lot of work by saying to that beast 'gee' and 'haw' instead of just jerking on the reins." The old-timer mopped his brow and replied, "Yep, I know. But this here mule done kicked me six years ago, and I ain't spoke to her since!"

"Words spoken with the right attitude can initiate healing in fractured relationships and put to rest simple disputes."

Let me encourage you to not wait for the other person to take the first step, even if they were in the wrong. You take that first step. If the problem is left unresolved, what could have been a short step will become an almost impossible leap. Jesus advised in Matthew 5:25, *"Agree with your adversary quickly...."* Such humility and willingness to admit our own wrongs will take us far in our journey to be salt in our families and in the world.

Day 12

The Buck Stops Where?
Matthew 5:26a

A practical step to having a salt-filled life is to realize where the buck does stop. We need to know what is expected of us and what we can expect from others. In this, we will experience confidence in what we do and attain a comfort level in associating with others.

When we find ourselves in discord with family, friends, superiors, or even lenders, it is often a result of poor communication. Good communication is when one's own understanding of their obligation parallels or matches that of the other person's expectation.

> *"We can be salt in our relationships with others by being dependable and trustworthy."*

Jesus talks about a person who neglected their responsibility in Matthew 5:26, *"I tell you the truth, you will not get out until you have paid the last penny"* (NIV). So whether we find ourselves in prison or in hot water, we still won't get away with shirking our responsibilities. Therefore, let's de- termine to communicate and get a good understanding of what, how, and when something is to be done. When an obligation has been carried out and lines up with expectation, we find a harmonious relationship. We can be salt in our relationships with others by being dependable and trustworthy.

Although we may not have responsibility flow charts and contracts between family and friends, let's take seriously these special people and consider their well-being above our own. With this attitude, we will desire a greater understanding of one another, resulting in salt-filled and enduring (preserved) relationships.

Day 13

Dealing with Debt
Matthew 5:26b

I have not yet broken the news to my 16 grandchildren that each one of them is $14,770 in debt. It's called the national debt. We are each paying a little, or perhaps a lot, towards it every time we turn around. However, our common debt is still an issue. Many of us are not so aware, or perhaps even concerned, about this national debt problem because we are finding it hard to see over our own personal debt.

In life, one of the main allies of stress is debt. We see stress and the results of it in marriage, the workplace, ministry, and the list goes on. The steps to getting out of debt are also sure steps to fulfill our call to be salt and light. There is exhaustive teaching available on this subject. Here are some interesting points for you to ponder.

It's all right to borrow money because there is a plan in place to pay it back. Where we get into trouble, and find the word "debt" takes on a sting, is when we borrow and are not able to meet our obligations. We may end up shirking our responsibilities or borrowing more money to deal with the present emergency. Then we become miserable and more in debt. However, let's not get discouraged – there is a way out.

Some of the steps may seem drastic, but drastic measures may be called for. The three areas we need to activate for the successful management of our debt are: 1) *Determination,* 2) *Understanding,* and 3) *Action.* With *determination,* we need to commit to getting out of debt. With *understanding,* we need to make a list of all our creditors and amount owing. And thirdly, with *action,* we need to set a plan in place for wise spending. Remember to look ahead for anticipated expenses such as tires, college, weddings, emergencies and retirement.

Continuing under action, we need to make a list of our assets and ask, "Is there anything I can sell or downscale?" Also, until spending is under control, we should only pay for services and products with cash. In addition, when trying to reduce debt, it is wise to avoid situations that you know encourage spending. Places such as shopping malls, car lots, etc.

Often by the time a person discovers that money doesn't grow on trees, they may already be way out on a limb. I heard a saying when I was a boy and have since repeated it several times. It goes like this, "If your Out-Go is more than your In-Come, then your Up-Keep will be your Down-Fall."

In regards to money, that great reformer John Wesley advised: "Make as much as you can. Save as much as you can. Give as much as you can." In other words, with what ability God has given us, we should make as good an income as possible and live a balanced lifestyle according to God's will. Then we should focus on our *needs* and not our *greeds*. And finally, we should put to great use that extra money and be a blessing to God's work and help those around us.

"In regards to money, that great reformer John Wesley advised: 'Make as much as you can. Save as much as you can. Give as much as you can.'"

Jesus explained in Matthew 5:26, *"...you will not get out until you have paid the last penny"* (NIV). He was referring to debtor's prison. You may not be behind bars but you may feel like it. Use the Master's key to get out and to continue as His salt and light with determination, understanding and action that is guided by the Spirit of God.

Day 14

Not "The Ten Suggestions"
Matthew 5:27

If you were to take a bowling ball, hold it above your head, and then let it go, you would experience the law of gravity in a very memorable way. There are other laws that, if disregarded, can hurt you more than a bowling ball ever could. They are best known as "The Ten Commandments."

The sooner we recognize The Ten Commandments as an imperative guide and rule to life, the sooner we can progress as salt of the earth. God not only gave us The Ten Commandments (Exodus 20:1-27), He also wrote them on the tablets of our hearts. We simply know them intrinsically.

1. You shall have no other gods before Me.
2. You shall not have any idols to worship.
3. You shall not take the name of the Lord in vain.
4. Remember the Sabbath day, to keep it holy.
5. Honour your father and your mother.
6. You shall not murder.
7. You shall not commit adultery.
8. You shall not steal.
9. You shall not bear false witness.
10. You shall not covet anything of your neighbour.

You may respond, "I can't deal with all of these; there are too many!" Well, Jesus explained that they can all be summed up this way: *"...love the Lord your God with all your heart, with all your soul, and with all your mind."* Then He continued, *"...and the second is like it.... You shall love your neighbour as yourself"* (Matthew 22:37-39). We won't have to worry about the *don'ts* if we concern ourselves with the *dos*.

Eric Liddell (featured in the movie, *Chariots of Fire)* participated in the 1924 Olympics, which were held in Paris. He was scheduled to run in the 100-metre dash on a Sunday but refused because it would violate his Christian convictions. A lot of pressure was brought to bear on him but he stayed true to his faith. One British official lamented,

"What a pity we couldn't have persuaded him to run." Liddell's coach thoughtfully replied, "No, it would have been a pity if we had because we would have separated him from the Source of his speed." Liddell had strong convictions. If he were to go against them, he would have lost some self-respect, even though he most likely would have won gold for that particular race. (Liddell actually won a gold medal in the 1924 Olympics for the 400-metre race instead!) We cannot go against what we know to be true if we want to experience a great impact on our nation.

God's nature is not changed by our opinion of Him. Yet people keep referring to "the God I believe in." It's all part of our culture's search for a permissive God. People today do not want a God who makes demands and interferes with their personal business, especially in the areas of sex and money.

We must have the right of choice, even to choose wrong, if we shall ever learn to choose right. The child walks as we unwind the swaddling cloths; the building stands in its full beauty as we remove the scaffolding.

Humankind has made more than 32 million laws that all branch back to The Ten Commandments. It would be a good idea to remember these "Top Ten," especially since our culture is continually pushing for greater moral licence.

When beginning to address a serious topic from The Ten Commandments, Jesus said, *"You have heard that it was said to those of old..."* (Matthew 5:27). He was bringing time-proven truths to His era, and to ours once again, validating for us the importance of The Ten Commandments as the written foundation of what is right and wrong.

The law is a good thing. It is like a dentist's little mirror which is placed into the patient's mouth. With the mirror he can detect any cavities, decayed areas, and other abnormalities. However, the dentist does not drill with it.

The law of gravity never punishes and, likewise, the laws of The Ten Commandments do not punish. They simply give precepts to live by. If we choose to disregard them, we incur the consequences, guilt, shame, conviction, and possible imprisonment.

Rather than being some sort of penalty, obedience is what makes faith strong. Far from being oppressive, the commandments are blessings. Our impact as salt will be unhindered if we understand the freedom and comfort within the law.

Day 15

Blinders
Matthew 5:28

Remember the movie titled, *The Ten Commandments?* Actor Charlton Heston portrays Moses ascending Mount Sinai where he has a personal encounter with the Living God. These are definitely not just ten suggestions, they are orders from the Almighty God. It's quite evident from Cecil B. DeMill's movie and, from our consciences, that the failure to observe these commandments brings consequences.

Years ago at Christmas, my wife Norma-Jean and I, along with our children and grandchildren, were given a horse named "Buster." The Amish farmer residing in St. Jacobs, Ontario, from whom Buster was purchased, assured me that this horse needed "blinders," especially when pulling the buggy into town. Without them, Buster may get into trouble. Surely, we humans don't need blinders, or do we? A lot of spark is lost when a faithful wife secs her husband ogle another woman or vice versa. Unless the conscience is calloused, the ogler also loses spark.

"...the failure to observe these commandments brings consequences."

I recall playing snakes and ladders with my grandson Adam several years ago. Whenever I would land on the snake, I would slide backwards. So it is with oglers. Instead of being "salty," it's a slide away from saltiness. *"But I say to you that whoever looks at a woman to lust for her has already committed adultery with her in his heart"* (Matthew 5:28). Yes, perhaps temporarily there is sensual pleasure, but our effectiveness soon disappears.

If you are married, strive through prayer, reading God's Word and dating to come to the point where you can say to your beloved one the words of that old song, *I Only Have Eyes For You.* Then you and your partner can help each other in your salt witness.

Day 16

The Surgical Cure
Matthew 5:29

From 1977 to 1992, *100 Huntley Street* originated from a building in the heart of Toronto with that same address. On my way to work for at least half of those years, I would travel north on Jarvis Street from the Gardiner Expressway. Almost every morning I would see garbage truck #100 and be reminded daily to make sure all of my life's garbage was put out in order to start a new day right.

Farther north on Jarvis Street was a billboard. That memory brings me to another preserving effect of salt. It was usually an advertisement for a car or some commodity accompanied by a scantily clad female model. I resent being bombarded with those public images which would make any red-blooded male react. Those reactions are to be reserved for the bedroom with one's own spouse. Whether in a magazine or on a billboard, any public display of nakedness or near nakedness does not help the observer to develop a healthy, loving relationship with their spouse. On the contrary, it can be like the thin edge of the wedge that divides. Also, the enticing trap of pornography destroys respect for the humanity of others and their sexuality. People become nothing more than objects to use and abuse and discard. This is one of the reasons why pornography is such a blight on humanity.

But there it was every morning, the huge well-lit billboard. If I kept my eye on the road, I couldn't miss it. What does one do? Soon the other side of the street became the focus of my attention. I found that I could drive past the billboard with only my peripheral vision covering the street immediately in front of my car. In effect, I was able to turn a blind eye to the billboard.

In Matthew 5:29, Jesus said in that common rabbinical teaching technique of overstatement, *"If your eye offends you, pluck it out."* Eventually my journey up Jarvis Street became happier and I moved farther along in my journey into being the salt of the earth. Jesus' disciple John explains it this way: *"Do not love the world or the things in the world. If anyone loves the world, the love of the Father is not in him. For all that is in the world – the lust of the flesh, the lust of the eyes, and the pride of life – is not of the Father but is of the world. And the world is passing away, and the lust of it; but he who does the will of God abides forever"* (1 John 2:15-17).

Drastic Measure
Matthew 5:30

The human hand is a marvellous thing. Consisting of 27 bones, it is the most versatile part of the human body. Agility is seen in the hands of a concert pianist, sensitivity is revealed when braille is read by the blind, and power is felt when a martial artist strikes a blow.

The hand can lovingly caress a tiny baby or it can clench into a fist and abuse a child or a spouse. The hand can give generously, even sacrificially, and yet it can steal. It can hold a hypodermic needle to give an injection that will save a life, or it can hold a gun to maim or murder. These hands can deliver a precious baby – the gift of life – or they can manipulate instruments or inject poison into the womb to take a life.

Years ago at Christmas time, my son-in-law Nizar Shaheen showed us all (including his wife and children) something we did not know about him. In a burst of joy, he walked all around the family room on his hands with his feet above his head. Our hands can do many delightful and incredible things. But how do we deal with a bad hand – an evil hand?

The solution of the world's greatest Teacher can be found in His most famous teaching, the Sermon on the Mount: *"... if your right hand causes you to sin, cut it off and cast it from you"* (Matthew 5:30a). Instead of doing wrong, handicap yourself. Rather than using a hand for evil, act as if it had been cut off. The hand should not bring about bad things, only good. Let's walk on our hands in our quest to remain salt and light.

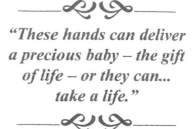

"These hands can deliver a precious baby – the gift of life – or they can... take a life."

Day 18

For Better, For Worse
Matthew 5:31

Marriage, the way God planned it, can be so fulfilling. If we assure one another of our love and commitment to a healthy marriage, we will experience a joy that will be infectious. Remember this phrase, "For better for worse; for richer for poorer; in sickness and in health; to love, honour and cherish, until death do us part"? Well, for most of us married couples, it is not too late to fulfill and renew that vow.

According to a former Gallup Poll, only 5 percent of marriages are dissolved due to physical abuse, 16 percent because of alcoholism, and 17 percent due to adultery. The overwhelming cause of divorce is incompatibility (47 percent) and arguments over money, family or children (10 percent). In other words, nearly 60 percent of all divorces are caused by poor communication. These marriages (and, yes, others too!) can be saved if both partners are willing to take an inventory of themselves and their marriage, and then make the necessary changes.

Years ago, Michael McManus, the creator of the Marriage Savers Resource Collection, was the guest of the week on *100 Huntley Street*. One of the issues we looked at was, "What's wrong with divorce?" We discovered much. There are four obvious wrongs brought by divorce.

1. *The most evident is the pain that divorce brings.* Even after ten years, it is reported that up to 90 percent of the divorced people are still experiencing pain. This comes as a surprise to many who feel that divorcing their spouse will allow them to get on with their lives. One woman was quoted as saying, "Divorce is like suffering death without a funeral. The pain never ends."

2. *Divorce is harmful to children.* The *Atlantic Monthly* magazine startled readers with an article announcing: "Dan Quayle was right." The article discusses the harm that children suffer from family breakdown. We certainly did not need Dan to tell us that. If we have eyes to see or ears to hear, we know it to be true. Children are perhaps the greatest casualty in a divorce. Broken families are the number one source for intellectual, physical and emotional scars. Also,

broken families contribute greatly to the drug crisis, the problems in our schools, teen pregnancy and juvenile crime. Most divorces lead to remarriage but to different spouses. And since 60 percent of remarriages fail, the odds are that a second divorce will occur before the children reach age 18.

3. Poverty is often the result of divorce. In the United States, youngsters living with one parent (usually their mothers) are six times as likely to be living at the poverty level than children who live with both parents. I'm sure the statistic for Canada is similar.

4. The fourth reason why divorce is wrong is that Scripture speaks strongly against it. The Old Testament writer Malachi predicts three negative consequences of divorce: great sorrow, distress, and that children of divorce are more likely to be rebellious. Malachi also states, *"For the Lord God of Israel says that He hates divorce"* (2:16a).

Malachi also writes that there is weeping and crying: *"...Because the Lord has been witness between you and the wife of your youth, with whom you have dealt treacherously; yet she is your companion and your wife by covenant. But did He not make them one, having a remnant of the Spirit? And why one? He seeks Godly offspring. Therefore take heed to your spirit, and let none deal treacherously with the wife of his youth"* (Malachi 2:14,15).

Jesus taught us how to live in peace. He also gave the best formula for a healthy marriage. He said, *"This is My commandment, that you love one another as I have loved you"* (John 15:12). Paul expounded on this in his letter to the Ephesians in chapter 5, where he gave couples two steps. If "Step A"(which is the man's responsibility) is in place, then "Step B" (which is the woman's responsibility) follows naturally. However, if "Step A" is not practised, the breakdown of the marriage occurs. Here is "Step A" from Paul's pen: *"Husbands, love your wives, just as Christ also loved the church and gave Himself for her"* (Ephesians 5:25). And here is "Step B," the natural response to a man with the kind of love that is revealed in Christ Jesus: *"Wives, submit to your own husbands."* In other words, let them lead.

Jesus spoke against divorce, only allowing it in the case of adultery. He also made this statement regarding a couple: *"...they are no longer two but one flesh. Therefore what God has joined together, let not man separate"* (Matthew 19:6). Let's retain our salty savour by being faithful and committed to one another.

Day 19

Mourn the Porn
Matthew 5:32

Marriage has been with us since the creation of man. Some have tried to make it a memorable event. For example, the Kearns got married 2,000 feet above the ground in a glider. The Zehnders got married in an ice cave in Antarctica. The Cardiffs got married 18,640 feet atop Mount Kilimanjaro in Africa. I even heard that a couple got married under water in scuba suits. Some have made it not such a memorable event. In 1988, 6,516 South Korean couples were married in one mass wedding. Some other interesting facts are: The Morans of Seattle have married each other 40 times, the Narimans of Bombay had the longest-recorded marriage of 86 years, the oldest groom was 103 and the oldest bride was one day short of 100. On the sad side of extremes, Mr. Glynn had been divorced and remarried 27 times, and the Sterns of Milwaukee divorced at their respectable ages of 91 and 97.

George Gallup Jr., Chairman of Gallup International Institute said, "If a disease were to afflict the majority of a populace, spreading pain and dysfunction throughout all age groups, we would be frantically searching for reasons and solutions." Mr. Gallup concludes his statement with words of truth, "The scourge is divorce."

"We need to guard against anything destructive that will impact our relationship with God and with our loved ones."

One of our *100 Huntley Street* guests, Dr. James Dobson, has been quoted: "Don't permit the possibility of divorce to enter your thinking. Even in moments of great conflict and discouragement, divorce is no solution." Divorce is usually an attempt to leave a set of problems. However, it usually inherits a whole lot more. The best resolve is to work through the problem with the person whom you vowed to love and honour.

In our journey as salt and light,

let's reassure one another of our love and commitment to a healthy marriage, and let's be willing to do whatever it takes to reconcile and repair the bonds of matrimony. We need to guard against anything destructive that will impact our relationship with God and with our loved ones. A major cause of destruction in a marriage is pornography. It separates a man from open intimacy with his wife. It is sad that this is very predominant in our sick society and has been the initial cause of many family breakups and many shed tears.

Producers of porn have distorted the meaning and purpose of sex and, as a result, have robbed many of the experience of pure sexual fulfillment. God meant it to be a beautiful gift that is full of wonder and mystery. Instead, pornography leads to sorrow and empty addiction. It separates loved ones and erodes society. It can push a person to rape or harm another person. The list goes on. Let's perceive it for what it is and have righteous anger towards this exploitation called pornography. In a society where much is disposable, marriage should not be on the disposable list. "Mourn the Porn" and take steps to dispose of everything hurtful to a healthy marriage. A healthy marriage will help both partners be salt to each other, and to the world.

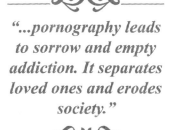

"...pornography leads to sorrow and empty addiction. It separates loved ones and erodes society."

Day 20

Consistency is a Rare Jewel
Matthew 5:34-37

As an 18-year-old, I was devastated by a layoff from the magnesium mine at Haley's Station, Ontario. It seemed that my plans to set aside enough money for university were ruined. How I prayed! You can imagine my surprise when I received a call from the inspector of the public schools based in Pembroke, asking me to consider a teaching position at the Chalk River Public School. What a shock. This was not in my plan, but I desperately needed a job.

I travelled up the Ottawa Valley for 37 miles in my '47 Plymouth. I visited the school and the chairman of the school board. I talked to adults, teens and children. The teens told me that the man who served as principal had been thrown out his own office window twice by the older boys. This job wasn't going to be easy by any stretch of the imagination. I learned that this volatile situation was the main reason they had decided to open a fourth classroom in an effort to reduce the number of students per teacher and hope for better things. It was intimidating to discover that I was the "hope" for improvement!

After much more prayer, I accepted. In great consternation I came to my father who had taught public school, served as a minister, missionary and college president. I asked him how I could receive respect and obedience from teens almost as old as I was. Dad's response was brief, and he didn't offer to expand on the six words of wisdom he offered. He said: "Consistency, thou art a rare jewel."

From that point on, I thought carefully about what I said before I said it. I mentioned it only once, making sure I was heard and understood. Then I backed up my word with consequences (good or bad, depending on the occasion or the circumstances). One young man, who should have been in high school but was still in Grade 6, was able to progress two years in six months. Today he is a successful businessman in British Columbia.

Jesus said, *"...let your 'Yes' be 'Yes,' and your 'No,' 'No.' Anything beyond this comes from the evil one."* The Lord is totally consistent. Whenever He inspired the prophets and the apostles to write His words down, you can count on it! His words will help you be salt in your life and in the world. So step forward boldly in your powerful saltiness by deciding to possess that rare jewel called consistency.

Day 21

We Shall Overcome
Matthew 5:38,39

Gandhi shook an empire with the moral superiority of his refusal to retaliate violently. This principle, when applied to our everyday personal lives is definitely the way to reconciliation between a husband and wife, parents and children, neighbours, churches, etc. This is a very important step to take in order to be truly salt and light in our world.

The ancient ethics were based on *"an eye for an eye, a tooth for a tooth."* This was a law of mercy to stop the murder of entire families, clans or tribes because of some injustice perpetrated by one person; a law to be enforced by a judge and not by vigilantes.

According to some experts, it was never literally carried out nor was it intended to be carried out. The law was likened to rabbinical teaching which often used exaggeration to make a point. Judges enforced a cash payment to the injured person, similar to what we do today. Jesus obliterated the very principal of that law in His Sermon on the Mount, as retaliation has no place whatsoever in the teachings of Jesus.

Martin Luther King's nonviolent protests changed the hearts and minds of millions. His dream is thus far unfulfilled but there was no mistaking the joy in the faces of those who sang, *We Shall Overcome.* That minister of the Gospel was salt indeed.

In October of 1990, I sat for breakfast in Moscow with five pastors from several of the Soviet Union republics. One of those pastors had a terribly crippled hand. At first, it looked like the worst case of arthritis I had ever seen. Yet, when I noticed that

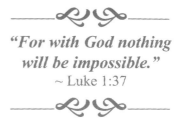

"For with God nothing will be impossible."
~ Luke 1:37

his other hand was fine, I knew it wasn't arthritis. So I asked him, through my interpreter, "What happened?" He answered, "I was in prison because I wouldn't stop telling people publicly about Jesus... they broke my fingers one at a time."

The amazing thing is that he was smiling as he told me this.

There was not a trace of bitterness. He continued: "They deliberately bound my hand so that when the bones did come back together, they would be grotesque as a reminder of what they thought was my foolishness. But that's okay, now they have actually asked my forgiveness. In fact, they have offered me a free trip to the hospital to rebreak my fingers and set them straight (this time under anesthetic)." His response to their request astonished them: "Of course, I forgive you, but I haven't got time for the operation. Besides, when I'm preaching and hold up my hand, it really gets the attention of the people."

Then to my surprise, there was this big belly laugh from all five of those pastors. There was no bitterness. These were truly Spirit-filled men. I felt like crawling under the table with my non-persecuted, North-American life. Even then, I would not be worthy to unloose their shoes. These men had a strong "saltiness" about them.

Jesus taught in Matthew 5:38-39: *"You have heard that was said, 'An eye for an eye and a tooth for a tooth.' But I tell you not to resist an evil person. But whoever slaps you on your right cheek, turn the other to him also."* It will not happen very often to us, if at all, that someone will slap us on the face. But time and time again, life brings us insults: little ones and sometimes big ones.

"The true followers of Jesus – the ones aspiring to be the salt of the earth – are really hard to offend since they have learned to endure and not seek retaliation."

The true followers of Jesus – the ones aspiring to be the salt of the earth – are really hard to offend since they have learned to endure and not seek retaliation. It may be humanly impossible but Jesus did say, *"For with God nothing will be impossible"* (Luke 1:37).

Facing Greed
Matthew 5:40,41

To be a giving person, one has to go through a process. We are all at some point in this process. The further along we get, the saltier we will be.

As children, we all had a bad case of the "gimmees." It wasn't something contagious that we caught from a runny-nosed kid. The "gimmees" just came with our human nature. We would demand, "Gimme this and gimme that." There we were, only two feet tall and feeling the world revolved around us. Mom or Dad were our loving servants who did everything for us and responded to our every whim or scream. We were the 'apple of their eyes,' and we knew it, often using that knowledge to our advantage. Then we grew up. Some of us, however, still make a fuss if we don't get our way or pout if we don't get the desired result. Even as adults, we can get defensive – and even offensive – over what we feel are our rights, no matter how insignificant the issue.

There is great freedom and joy to be found as we release this attitude that 'the world *owes* me,' and begin to realize that 'the world *needs* me.' How much happier this world would be if we had more givers than takers. Being salt means being a giver.

I have heard it said, "We make a living by what we get, but we make a life by what we give." Giving is an important ingredient in having a joyful life. I have never heard of, or met, a happy miser or a joyful tightwad. However, I do remember encountering life-filled, joyous people who considered it a privilege and a joy to give of themselves and their resources to make a positive difference in the lives of others.

In the *Guinness Book of World Records,* Hettie Green is described as the "most miserly miser." In the early 1900s, she lived on cold oatmeal, not wanting to spend or give away her precious money. She left 95 million dollars when she died. Just think of the enduring

"How much happier this world would be if we had more givers than takers. "
~ Luke 1:37

legacy she could have provided if she had focussed on contributing to the needs of others around her. She would have been remembered in a far better way.

In the crucifixion of Jesus we see the supreme example of giving. Jesus taught us how we ought to give, even when it is demanded of us. He said in Matthew 5:40-41, *"If anyone wants to sue you and take away your tunic, let him have your cloak also. And whoever compels you to go one mile, go with him two."*

Let's continue on our journey of salt and light by recognizing others and helping to meet their needs. We can be there for each other by showing kindness, love and generosity.

"Let's continue on our journey of salt and light by recognizing others and helping to meet their needs. We can be there for each other by showing kindness, love and generosity."

Day 23

Unconditional Love
Matthew 5:43-48

When we have our own personal antagonist – a person who does something or says something to hurt us intentionally – it is very easy and natural for us to put them in the category of "enemy." However, that attitude is quite self-destructive. To have an enemy is to also have turmoil, anxiety, hatred and bitterness. And to have these emotions is not typical of being salt and light. We can get on in our journey as we recognize our need of supernatural love from above.

Corrie Ten Boom shares this true story in her book, *The Hiding Place:*

> "It was a church service in Munich that I saw him, the former S.S. man who had stood guard at the shower room door in the processing centre at Ravensbruck. He was the first of our actual jailers that I had seen since that time. And suddenly it was all there – the roomful of mocking men, the heaps of clothing, (sister) Betsie's pain-blanched face. He came up to me as the church was emptying, beaming and bowing. 'How grateful I am for your message, Fraulein,' he said. 'To think that, as you say, He has washed my sins away!' His hand was thrust out to shake mine.

> "And I, who had preached so often to the people in Bloemendaal, the need to forgive, kept my hand at my side. Even as the angry, vengeful thoughts boiled through me, I saw the sin of them. Jesus Christ had died for this man; was I going to ask for more? 'Lord Jesus,' I prayed, 'forgive me and help me to forgive him.' I tried to smile, I struggled to raise my hand. I could not. I felt nothing, not the slightest spark of warmth or charity. And so again I breathed a silent prayer. 'Jesus, I cannot forgive him. Give me Your forgiveness.' As I took his hand, the most incredible

thing happened. From my shoulder, along my arm and through my hand, a current seemed to pass from me to him, while into my heart sprang a love for this man that almost overwhelmed me. And so I discovered that it is not on our forgiveness any more than on our goodness that the world's healing hinges, but on His. When He tells us to love our enemies, He gives, along with the command, the love itself."

It was prayer and determination that brought Corrie Ten Boom to experience a supernatural love for this man – the same man who had participated in exterminating her family and friends.

Yes, Jesus did say those words – *"love your enemies."* He wasn't talking about the kind of love that we have for our family and for close friends. Jesus was exhorting us about "agape" love. This love is full of benevolence and goodwill. Agape love means that no matter what that person does to us – no matter how he treats us, no matter if he insults us or injures us or grieves us – we will never allow any bitterness against him to invade our hearts. Instead, we will seek nothing but the highest good for that person. To have agape love is to have the power to love those whom we do not like and who may not like us. This is because of the life of Christ living in us, helping us to become salt.

"When He [Jesus] tells us to love our enemies, He gives, along with the command, the love itself."

Can we pray for our enemies? That is the acid test to know if we truly do love our enemies. And in prayer, our ability to love them will grow even more. As we determine that love will prevail, we will find love. And we will be saltier than ever!

Day 24

The Salt of Blessing
Matthew 5:43-48

To return cursing for cursing is not an honourable thing. However, to be able to hold the tongue or, better yet, not feel the urge to retaliate but respond in kindness is a great thing. *"A soft answer turns away wrath..."* (Proverbs 15:1). This is a wise truth that we need to act upon. And it is a daily, practical example of how we can be salt in very trying situations. We can take a solid step in our journey if we determine not to let our impact be dampened by an angry word aimed at us. To meet evil with evil is self-destructive and will bring us as low as the person who was out to hurt us.

When Leonardo da Vinci was painting that famous masterpiece known as "The Last Supper," he had an intense and bitter argument with a fellow painter. Leonardo was so enraged that he decided to paint the face of his enemy into the face of Judas. That way, the hated painter's face would be preserved for ages in the face of the betraying disciple. When Leonardo finished Judas, everyone easily recognized the face of the painter with whom Leonardo quarrelled. Leonardo continued to work on the painting. But as much as he tried, he could not paint the face of Christ. Something was holding him back.

He realized his hatred toward his fellow painter was the problem. So he worked through his hatred by repainting Judas' face, replacing the image of his fellow painter with another face. Only then was he able to paint Jesus' face and complete the masterpiece.

A number of years ago at the Hamilton YMCA, there was a young man that I was trying to help. He had messed up his life with drug addiction. On one occasion when I walked in his room to visit him, I found him with his face in a paper bag that had glue smeared on the inside at the bottom. He was sniffing glue to get high. I tried to get his attention by talking to him and saying things like, "Jesus really

"...to be able to hold the tongue or, better yet, not feel the urge to retaliate but respond in kindness is a great thing."

loves you, Gord." He responded by lifting his face from that bag just long enough to spit right in my face. What a shock! I was surprised that I didn't react by grabbing him by the throat. What happened was (and this was not me) the tears began to flow and mingle with the spit. It was the heart of Jesus actually reacting through me!

Jesus said in Luke 6:28, *"Bless those who curse you."* This is only possible if our wellspring, the fountain within, is flowing with love; a supernatural love from above that God puts in every willing heart. When you assess how you typically respond, do you feel that you could use more of that kind of love? Could you be saltier? God can bring you to a place in your life where you begin to see people – yes, even adversaries – through Jesus' eyes. The Lord can also fill you with His Spirit so that you can respond as the Spirit of God would respond. To bless those who curse you is a tall order, but with Him all things are possible!

"Jesus taught, 'Pray for those who spitefully use you...' (Luke 6:28). Try it. It will make more room in your life to be salt and light."

122

Day 25

Praying Through Me
Matthew 5:43-48

A vivid memory that often comes to my mind took place in Canada's capital city of Ottawa. I was 12 when my mother died. My father and I were in his 1948 Chevrolet as we pulled away from the curb in front of the funeral home and turned onto Bank Street. For two or three blocks we remained silent while tears welled up in our eyes. Dad thoughtfully reflected, "In all our lives together, I've never heard your mother say anything bad about anybody." Then silence reigned again. As I think back on her life, she was a happy person. I can remember several of her hilarious April Fool's Day stunts, but my most persistent memory is seeing her on her knees in prayer. This was the secret of her joy and her ability to say either kind things about people or nothing at all.

In New Orleans during 1960, a federal judge ruled that the city schools must be integrated. A six-year-old girl, Ruby Bridges, was the only black child to attend the William T. Frantz School. Every day for weeks, as she entered and left the building, a mob would be standing outside to scream at her and threaten her. They shook their fists, shouted obscenities, and threatened to kill her. One day, Ruby's teacher saw her lips moving as she walked through the crowd, flanked by burly federal marshals. The teacher asked Ruby if she was talking to the people. "I wasn't talking to them," she replied. "I was just saying a prayer for them." The teacher then asked her, "Why did you do that?" "Because they need praying for," came her reply. What a salt presence Ruby was!

When Job's three so-called friends ridiculed him with harsh and untrue words, Job proved to be an overcomer. At the very end of the book of Job it says, "After Job had prayed for his friends, the Lord made him prosperous again and gave him twice as much as he had before." (Job 42:10 NIV).

Jesus taught, *"Pray for those who spitefully use you..."* (Luke 6:28). Try it. It will make more room in your life to be salt and light.

Wrong Motives
Matthew 6:1

A boy asked his mother, "May I be a preacher when I grow up?" She responded, "I suppose you can, but are you sure that's what you want to be?" He answered thoughtfully with these words: "Well, I've got to go to church anyhow. And since I hate to sit still and be quiet, I'd rather go to church and stand up and holler." Well, the boy sought something honourable, however, his motives were self-serving.

It's a good practice to slow down long enough to ask, "Why do I do what I do?" I'm sure we have all been guilty of doing the right things for the wrong reasons. We may give a gift, say a kind word, do a good deed (even preach, pray or fast) with an ulterior, self-seeking motive. Instead, we should be compelled by love for God and compassion for others.

Our motives are often a clouded area. To be the salt of the earth, we need to clear those clouds. This will be done by prayerful introspection and perhaps also counsel. Then we will better understand our motives and have them purified, resulting in newfound effectiveness.

It is a strange fact that good works can readily lend themselves to wrong motives. Often these things are done with the sole intention of bringing glory to the doer. A person may give money, not really to help the person to whom he gives, but simply to demonstrate his own generosity and bask in the warmth of someone's gratitude. A person may pray in such a way that their prayer is not really addressed to God, but to whoever may happen to be listening.

"Jesus addressed this concern in Matthew 6:1: 'Take heed that you do not do your charitable deeds before men, to be seen by them. Otherwise you have no reward from your Father in heaven.'"

Praying may simply be an attempt to demonstrate exceptional piety in such a way that no one can fail to see it. A person may fast, not really for the good of his own soul or to humble himself in the sight of God, but simply to show the world what a splendidly self-disciplined character he is. A person may practise good works simply to win praise from others, increase his own prestige, and show the world how good he is.

Jesus addressed this concern in Matthew 6:1: *"Take heed that you do not do your charitable deeds before men, to be seen by them. Otherwise you have no reward from your Father in heaven."*

You may feel insecure, have low self-esteem, be weighted down by guilt, or experience fear. This may be the result of being mistreated during your younger years, creating the need for a continual striving in order to feel good about yourself. Being self-centred is usually associated with the prideful person, but it is also descriptive of someone who is in a self-preservation mode or one who desires to prove to the world – and to themselves – that they are special. If some of this is lining up with your life, then there are underlying reasons that must be dealt with and rooted out so you can be motivated by love for God and others.

Understanding our motives and taking the necessary action towards having pure motives is an important step in our journey. We need to realize that self-centredness will destroy relationships, take our focus off God and prevent us from seeing the needs of others. Kingdom effectiveness flows from right relationships – first with God and next with our fellowman. If your life is fueled by love, there will be more joy in giving than receiving. First and foremost, we need to give to bless the recipient rather than ourselves.

A writer for a great newspaper once visited India. While there, he met a missionary nurse who lived among the lepers and ministered to their needs. He noticed how tender and loving she was to those poor souls. Looking at her in amazement, the reporter commented, "I wouldn't wash their wounds for a million dollars!" "Neither would I," replied the Christian worker, "but I would gladly do it for my Saviour. The only reward I'm looking for is His smile of approval." We need to share the motive the missionary had, and that is the smile of God's approval! Imagine the impact of being salt like that!

Day 27

Don't Blow Your Own Horn
Matthew 6:2-4

There is a cute story about a little boy who followed the church treasurer every Sunday morning as the man carried the offering out of the auditorium. The boy would watch the man intently, count the offering and put it in the safe. At first the treasurer ignored him, but after several weeks he finally asked, "Son, why do you follow me around every Sunday?" The boy looked up at the treasurer and replied, "The preacher says that the offering is for God, and I want to see you give it to Him!"

What would it be like if we could literally see the Lord and place our offerings directly into His hands? Would our motives for giving change? Would we give more than we usually do? Would we be more cheerful in our giving? For those who presently give out of obligation, conviction, or the need for approval, giving directly to God would have an altering effect; a complete overhaul in their giving. There would be dramatic changes in motives, in attitudes, and in the amount given.

Yet this unsettling scenario is reality. If we look with our spiritual eyes of faith, we will see that whenever we give from a heart of love, we give to the Lord. This step in our journey of salt and light is twofold. The first step is to find joy in pleasing God. And the second is finding joy in knowing that He sees in secret and rewards openly.

"The first step is to find joy in pleasing God. And the second is finding joy in knowing that He sees in secret and rewards openly."

Jean Frederic Oberlin, a celebrated Lutheran minister in 18th-century Germany, encountered a person who had this servant attitude. It was winter and Oberlin was travelling by foot when a severe snowstorm engulfed the countryside. He soon lost his way in the blowing snow and feared he would freeze to death. In despair he sat down, not knowing which way to turn. Just then, a man passing by in a wagon saw Oberlin and rescued him. He took the minister to the next village and made sure he would be cared for. As the rescuer prepared to leave, Oberlin said, "Tell me your name so that I may at least have you in grateful remembrance before God." The man who by now had recognized Oberlin replied: "You are a minister. Please tell me the name of the good Samaritan." Oberlin said, "I cannot do that, for it is not given in the Scriptures." To this the man responded, "Until you can tell me his name, please permit me to withhold mine."

Jesus gave us this advice in Matthew 6:2-4: *"Therefore, when you do a charitable deed, do not sound a trumpet before you as the hypocrites do in the synagogues and in the streets, that they may have glory from men. Assuredly, I say to you, they have their reward. But when you do a charitable deed, do not let your left hand know what your right hand is doing, that your charitable deed may be in secret; and your Father who sees in secret will Himself reward you openly."* Cultivating humility is essential for those who want to become pure and "refined" salt.

"But when you do a charitable deed, do not let your left hand know what your right hand is doing, that your charitable deed may be in secret; and your Father who sees in secret will Himself reward you openly."

~ Matthew 6:3,4

Day 28

Conditional Forgiveness
Matthew 6:14,15

Two words, which on the surface sound like the opposite of saltiness, are really steps into being effective salt. Those words are, "I'm sorry." Many times this father of four and grandfather of 16 has needed the wisdom of Solomon to resolve disputes. As a father, I had the authority to order an apology – or else! As a grandfather, I don't have the same authority and must use all the tricks I've got to produce the same results. Now, with a little more patience on my part, along with a dose of humour and funny faces, the grandchildren will say (with a little grin already beginning to form), "I'm sorry." Two minutes later, it's over and the fun begins. As adults, it's a more difficult step and the process takes longer, but it still works wonders.

This business of forgiving others and being forgiven is serious stuff. And it's integral to being salt. Jesus said in Matthew 6:14-15: *"For if you forgive men their trespasses, your Heavenly Father will also forgive you. But if you do not forgive men their trespasses, neither will your Father forgive your trespasses."*

I remember an occasion that took place shortly after our family moved to the little village of Madoc, Ontario. I was in Grade 5 and the new kid at school. Some boys taunted and teased me. They said, "Mainse, you don't have the guts to steal an apple from Kincaid's grocery store." I responded, "Yes, I do." And sure enough, I did. Well, I thought I had destroyed the evidence on the way home. When I got in the door of my house, my mother was there to greet me. She had the ability to read me like a book. All it took was one look at my face and body language to reveal my guilt. Intuitively, she asked, "David, what's wrong?" "Oh, Mother, nothing!" I responded. She persisted, "Now, David, you're covering up something with a lie." Isn't it true how human nature can take a bad situation and make it worse? Stealing an apple was wrong,

"This business of forgiving others and being forgiven is serious stuff. And it's integral to being salt."

but covering it up with a lie only made it worse.

Eventually with her cross-examination, I broke down and started to cry. This nine-year-old finally spoke the truth: "I stole an apple from Kincaid's grocery store." Mother took me into my bedroom and got me down on my knees in the same location where I said my nighttime prayers. She knelt with me as I asked God to forgive me for stealing the apple and for lying. After praying and feeling much better, Mother firmly announced, "You must take money out of your own little bank to pay for that apple, and then ask for Mr. Kincaid's forgiveness."

Now, apples in those days were only five cents but to a child that was a lot. This was really one of the toughest things I've ever done in my life. So I took ten cents out, thinking that would make Mr. Kincaid feel a little better toward me. The more I thought about it, the harder it was to plan what I was to say. Instead, I sat down and wrote him a little note. I put the note in an envelope and addressed the outside, "Mr. Kincaid."

I still have the vivid memory of going into Kincaid's grocery store. On the counter was a Corn Flakes™ box. Well, I quickly shoved the little note under that box with the ten cents included. I was home only for about half an hour when the telephone rang. Mother answered it and gave me an anxiety attack when I heard her say his name. Mr. Kincaid wanted to speak to David Mainse. I thought I was in real trouble now. "David," said Mr. Kincaid, "that's the bravest thing I've ever seen a boy do. In fact, I need a boy to deliver groceries. Would you consider a job?" I don't recommend you try this as a way to get employment, but I do recommend asking for forgiveness in order to step into the direction of being the salt of the earth.

"For if you forgive men their trespasses, your Heavenly Father will also forgive you. But if you do not forgive men their trespasses, neither will your Father forgive your trespasses."

~ Matthew 6:14-15

Day 29

Don't Get Ahead of Yourself
Matthew 6:25-34

John Curtis, founder and director of the University of Wisconsin Stress Management Institute, came to this conclusion: "I believe 90 percent of stress is brought on by not living in the present moment, but by worrying about what's already happened, what's going to happen, or what could happen."

My wife Norma-Jean and I remember on several occasions being roused in the middle of the night from a restful sleep by one of our children who had a bad dream. In desperation, my little one would race into the bedroom, leap in the air and land with a bounce between us on our bed. Talk about rude awakenings! While trying to get over that heart-accelerating experience, we noticed it wouldn't take long before our child was soon fast asleep.

Children and adults alike can be hurt by the past and feel uncertain about the future. However, in the same way a child enters perfect rest in the arms of a parent, we also can enter into perfect rest as we recognize that God wants to be our Heavenly Father. Knowing this, we must determine to trust Him no matter how bleak the future looks.

It is said that there are two days that can rob you of all the good things that today can bring. Those two days are: *yesterday* and *tomorrow*. There are the regrets of yesterday and the worries of tomorrow. God would have us learn from our yesterdays and prayerfully plan for our tomorrows, but He emphasizes in Matthew 6:34 that we are to take life one day at a time.

There was an older gentleman who began cutting trees to construct a log house. A neighbour who knew his purpose and age asked him, "Isn't that too large an undertaking for one person who is no longer young?" The elderly man replied with this explanation: "It would be, if I looked beyond the chopping of the trees and sawing of logs, and pictured myself laying the foundation, erecting the walls and putting on the roof. Carrying that load all at once would exhaust me. But it isn't much of a job to cut down this little tree, and that's all I have to do right now." Now there's a man who knows how to live out that Biblical principal Jesus taught of living in the present.

Worry often gives a small thing a big shadow. Don't be overshadowed. Instead, let the calming presence of the Lord settle you as you place your trust in a Sovereign God and take life one day at a time. When you are not worrying, you can concentrate more on being salt.

Day 30

Ask, Seek, Knock
Matthew 7:7-11

There is joy when we ask for something and receive it. There is joy when we seek something and find it. There is also joy when we knock at the door of opportunity and it opens. How can we be sure that we are making the right request, or looking in the right place, or knocking on the right door?

A story is told about a man who got a permit to open the first tavern in a small town. The members of a local church were strongly opposed to the bar, so they began to pray, asking God to intervene. A few days before the tavern was scheduled to open, lightning hit the structure and it burned to the ground. The people of the church were surprised but pleased, until they received notice that the would-be tavern owner was suing them. He contended that their prayers were responsible for the burning of the building. They denied the charge. At the conclusion of the preliminary hearing, the judge remarked, "At this point, I don't know what my decision will be, but it seems that the tavern owner believes in the power of prayer and these church people don't."

When the Apostle Peter was put into prison, a group of Christians met to pray for his release. When they were told that Peter was knocking at their door, they didn't believe it. We are often like those first-century Christians. We pray, but really don't expect much to happen.

Jesus exhorts us in Matthew 7:7-11: *"Ask, and it will be given to you; seek, and you will find; knock, and it will be opened to you. For everyone who asks receives, and he who seeks finds, and to him who knocks it will be opened. Or what man is there among you who, if his son asks for bread, will give him a stone? Or if he asks for a fish, will he give him a serpent? If you then, being evil, know how to give good gifts to your children, how much more will your Father who is in heaven give good things to those who ask Him!"*

We can come to God as children come to their father. So let's be confident and not backward or shy in making our requests known to God. And let's not forget to ask Him to help make us salt! For that's what He intends us to be!

Appendix B

During the "salt project," we spoke to over 600 Christian leaders in more than 20 different communities across Canada. After commencing 25 meetings, we returned home with several hundred pages of notes. In the process of reviewing them, we learned a lot. We invite you to take a few moments to consider your own answers to the following four questions. If you would like to share your answers with us, we would love to hear from you. Please contact us by e-mail at: davidmainse@crossroads.ca

1. How did Jesus model His salt message?
    (Matthew 5:13)

2. What is the balance of the prophetic role of the Church in culture and the call to be loving and kind?

3. As it is believed best for the Church not to endorse specific political parties or candidates, please respond to this question: What are the rights and responsibilities of the Church in the political process?

4. In the balance of the prophetic role of the practical application of truth to daily life, what can the pastors, shepherds, spiritual fathers and mothers do to reverse the moral and social deconstruction of our historical Christian values?

SPECIAL NOTE: Visit www.crossroads.ca for further ministry resources and a "salt" biography of David Mainse in the "About Us" section.